D1371542

Seminar on the Acquisition
of Latin American Library Materials

Bibliography and Reference Series, 26

Suzanne Hodgman
Executive Secretary

Barbara Valk
Chair, Editorial Board

South American Population Censuses Since Independence

An Annotated Bibliography of Secondary Sources

Karin Simoneau

SALALM Secretariat
Memorial Library, University of Wisconsin-Madison

Contents

Preface vii

Introduction xi

Bibliography 1

    General sources 3

    Argentina 11

    Bolivia 21

    Brazil 25

    Chile 35

    Colombia 41

    Ecuador 47

    Guyana 49

    Paraguay 50

    Peru 51

    Surinam 57

    Uruguay 57

    Venezuela 60

Author Index 67

Preface

This is a bibliography of works that discuss South American demographic censuses since independence. Its purpose is simply to fill a perceived gap in the reference literature. Bibliographies of Latin American censuses already exist, but few are annotated, and are in any case merely lists of censuses and do not include non-governmental sources on the subject. In addition, most are out of date. Indexes, however well arranged and annotated, have their own limitations: they are far from complete; they are cumbersome to use; and even in the most specialized ones references on any particular topic have to be hunted for and extracted from a jungle of extraneous material. For these and other reasons an annotated, subject specific bibliography is an essential tool in facilitating research, and it is this need that the present work hopes to meet.

The bibliography was compiled at the UCLA Research Library, and inevitably it reflects to some extent the nature of the library's holdings. As noted below, indexes helped fill in some of the gaps and account for a large portion of the citations listed, particularly the very recent ones. Methodologically, the compilation proceeded along several lines, some more productive than others: (1) Two indexes turned out to be particularly fruitful sources, *Population Index* [1] and *Resúmenes sobre población en América Latina.* [2] Both are subject specific, focusing on demography, and both provide easy subject access because of the way the general field has been broken down into narrow, systematically arranged topics. They differ in other ways: *Population Index* covers a considerably longer period, an advantage lessened by the fact that in the earlier volumes coverage of South America is quite limited. Its geographical span is worldwide; its annotations are often short and sometimes lacking altogether. *Resúmenes . . .*, published by the Centro Latinoamericano de Demografía (see below), is a reference tool of the highest quality and, because of its regional focus and its comprehensive and up-to-date coverage, was of primary importance for locating recent sources for this bibliography. All the entries have very extensive annotations, apparently written by subject specialists, and include a listing of subject terms, which increases the ease of use. It did not begin publication until 1977. Other indexes were consulted as well, but turned out to be of only limited usefulness. (2) Bibliographies in published books and articles yielded a number of references. Unfortunately, in the case of many Latin American

---

[1] *Population Index.* V. 1- , 1935- . Princeton, N.J.: Office of Population Research, Princeton University, and the Population Association of America.

[2] *Resúmenes sobre población en América Latina. Latin American Population Abstracts.* V. 1- , 1977- . Santiago, Chile: Centro Latinoamericano de Demografía.

publications, the bibliographic information was sometimes incomplete and could not be verified independently. (3) UCLA's on-line catalog, ORION, was primarily of value for bibliographic verification and for identifying additional works by known authors, but also for limited subject searching.

Within the constraints of the above resources it is hoped that the bibliography at hand, although certainly not complete, is comprehensive enough to serve as a research tool of some usefulness for its chosen topic.

Scope. The bibliography lists works dealing with demographic censuses taken in the twelve South American republics since they achieved independence. For most of these nations (with the exception of Guyana and Surinam which became independent countries only recently) this theoretically means a time span beginning with the early years of the nineteenth century, but in fact all the references that were located date from after 1850. The bibliography is restricted to publications that actually discuss, however briefly, the censuses themselves, their history, methodology, objectives, the circumstances under which they were taken, etc., and thus it includes both official census documents as well as books and articles by individuals and public and private organizations. Census publications which are mere tabulations of figures are not listed. Also included are works analyzing census results in a general way, leaving out the vast number of studies which, although based on census figures, actually focus on a specific demographic subfield, such as mortality or internal migration. Not all the censuses included are national in scope. Local censuses, especially for earlier periods or for less statistically developed countries, are often all there is, and in addition to being valuable sources of demographic information they can shed light on the state of statistics in a country. Besides, local censuses are sometimes very well documented, as is the case with some early municipal and provincial censuses in Argentina. Test censuses are another, more recent form of the limited census as a result of new statistical procedures being developed.

Arrangement. The organization of the bibliography reflects one of its aims, which is to provide an overview of the published output on the subject, not just in terms of quantity but also when, where, and by whom. Consequently the most logical arrangement was judged to be by country, with chronological subdivisions, listing the citations within each subdivision alphabetically by author. Ten-year periods were chosen, partly because that has come to be the internationally accepted interval between censuses, and partly because a shorter period would be less clearly indicative of the amount of printed output for any given time. The alphabetical listing by author within each subdivision is based on the compiler's opinion that having works by a single author listed together is more important than strict chronology, and that in any case dates of publication are often fortuitous, having more to do with extraneous factors than with anything else.

Citation form. The entries follow a modified version of the *Chicago Manual of Style*. In entries with more than one author the names have been separated by a semicolon in order to avoid the confusion that may be caused by cases of multiple surnames for each author. Portuguese compound surnames have generally been listed by the last element, following library cataloging practice, except when the individual's preference dictated otherwise. Spanish surnames are listed by the first element. Capitalization in the non-English works was found to be very inconsistent and here has been reduced to a minimum. Thus it does not necessarily reflect the original usage. When the publisher and the author are the same, as is usually the case with official statistical agencies, the publisher's name has been omitted to reduce repetition. Because their titles indicated that they might be of interest, several mimeographed works, listed as "(Mimeo.)", were included, as were a few items whose citations are somewhat less complete than the standard format. They were not available for review, and the bibliographic information could not be independently verified. Cross-references have been used sparingly and are limited to a few items which bear a clear relationship to one another, such as a commentary on one author's work by another. When a citation is not followed by a summary of its content, the work either could not be obtained for review or the title was considered self-explanatory. Abbreviations and acronyms have been avoided as far as possible as a matter of principle.

Introduction

The traditional sources of demographic data for South America, as for most regions, are the records of vital statistics (births, deaths, marriages) and the population censuses. The two types of sources, although complementary, differ in nature and objective, the former recording population changes, the latter providing a static picture of a population at a particular point in time, a kind of demographic snapshot. From the time of the conquest through the third quarter of the eighteenth century, demographic censuses in the modern sense did not exist in South America, that is, censuses carried out with the deliberate intention of counting the population for demographic purposes.[3] Limited local counts were sporadically undertaken, usually by the secular authorities for specific reasons (fiscal, administrative, military), occasionally by the church for its own purposes.

The region continued in this essentially non-statistical stage until 1775, when the first census was taken in Cuba. During the next two years, on the order of the Spanish Crown, censuses were carried out all over Spanish America, and by coincidence similar counts were undertaken in Portugal's American colonies by local priests. The transition to the statistical period had been initiated. Censuses began to be taken intermittently in the region's more advanced provinces (and, after the independence movements of the early 1800s, self-governing countries), varying in regularity and reliability according to national resources and the efficiency of the government bureaucracy.

After the second half of the nineteenth century, South America can be considered to have truly entered the statistical phase. Civil registers of vital statistics began to be established, principally for juridical and administrative purposes. Several countries began to take censuses on a fairly regular basis. As a result of the beginnings of industrialization and economic development the objectives of the census taking were broadened and the scope of the information requested of the population expanded. The censuses were by now carried out exclusively by governments, national or local. Still, variability has remained a regional characteristic, both within and between countries. Thus Chile undertook its first census in 1832 and has taken one practically every decade since, whereas Ecuador did not take its first population census until 1950. Venezuela took its first modern census in 1873 and has carried out ten subsequent enumerations, giving it one of the more complete census records in the region. Argentina, despite its strong statistical tradition and its several well-administered and well-documented local

---

[3]Nicolás Sánchez-Albornoz, *The Population of Latin America: A History* (Berkeley and Los Angeles: University of California Press, 1974), 10.

censuses in the nineteenth century, has a spotty record with regard to national censuses. Although generally speaking there is a clear overall movement in South America toward greater regularity and accuracy of censuses, there are numerous exceptions. Sánchez-Albornoz notes that the first national censuses were clearly inferior in quality to the last colonial ones, owing to the collapse of the civil service in the tumult of the early nineteenth century.[4] Likewise, the 1960 census round is considered less reliable in some respects than some earlier censuses.

Guyana (formerly British Guiana) and Surinam (formerly Dutch Guiana), which achieved independence only in 1966 and 1975 respectively, are anomalous on the subcontinent. Lacking the common Iberian cultural heritage which connects their neighbors, and with a different ethnic make-up, they have limited ties with the rest of South America. The census history of Surinam is shallow indeed, even when the colonial period is considered. The first population census did not take place until 1950. One census has been taken since independence. For Guyana the record is considerably better, in that censuses were taken every decade, with a couple of exceptions, since 1861. Its censuses since 1966 have been carried out as part of the Census Research Programme of the University of the West Indies.

The situation in the region today is still far from uniform. Some countries, like Colombia and Brazil, have strong, well-staffed national statistical agencies with a mandate to carry out demographic research, whereas in other countries, for many reasons, the commitment is much less certain. International cooperation has long been an important factor. Earlier in this century, for example, the first and second conferences of the Pan American Scientific Congress concerned themselves with censuses and census problems. The Inter-American Statistical Institute has contributed greatly to furthering the cause of census taking and improving the quality of the data, as demonstrated by the so-called Census of the Americas (COTA) program that began in 1950. The Centro Latinoamericano de Demografía (CELADE) is a mainstay of demographic research in Latin America today. Founded in 1957 by the United Nations and the government of Chile, this organization has three main objectives: to carry out basic demographic research, to teach demography to Latin American students, and to advise their governments on technical matters in undertakings such as censuses. It proceeds enthusiastically on all three fronts, and the results include a stream of generally high-quality publications and the excellent *Resúmenes sobre población en América Latina*, mentioned above. Another statistical agency is the U.N. Economic Commission for Latin America (ECLA). Although not concerned with demographic research it takes an active part in assisting regional governments in organizing censuses and evaluating their results. Taken together, these three institutions have helped to raise the level of statistical development in those countries which already have a statistical tradition, and have assisted in establishing national census programs where such a tradition was weak or lacking.

A natural by-product of cooperation is greater uniformity. Census taking in South America has indeed grown increasingly standardized, in criteria, objectives, and information sought, and in the evaluation and processing of data. Computerization is of course a major

---

[4]Ibid., 9.

factor. Better quality control is also facilitated by new procedures such as sampling and test censuses.

The state of demography in the region today is the result of specific factors as well as generalized socio-cultural conditions, some of which will continue to affect the field in the foreseeable future. Certain events have occurred that have had a positive effect, such as the exile to South America earlier in the century of prominent European social scientists like the Italians Giorgio Mortara and Gino Germani. Increased international cooperation, as mentioned above, has also contributed positively. However, problems remain. Economic hardship, more severe in some countries than others, is a chronic factor. Social and political instability likewise inhibit census taking, which is usually a function of a relatively stable society. Conflicting international boundary claims sometimes constitute a problem. Another constraint until the recent past has been the unfortunate prevalence in the region of political dictatorships: military strong-men tend to regard social scientists with some suspicion and have little interest in the social reality around them. In addition, to quote Mortara, "in most Latin American countries, the inefficiency of public administrations, added to the lack of civic-mindedness [and] the widespread ignorance and poverty of the citizens, makes reliable censuses difficult."[5] Further complications include populations spread over frequently remote, rugged areas accessible only with great difficulty, and, in the actual census process itself, occasional fraudulent manipulation of data by local officials.

Accentuating these problems has been a great scarcity of trained demographers. This has only recently begun to change, in large part because of the activities of CELADE, but the problem is to some extent culturally conditioned and can best be understood in its broader context. Latin American culture is at least in part the product of a non-empirically based, humanistically focused education. From the earliest age through university it fosters a cultural tradition which until recently has been primarily oriented toward letters, philosophy, rhetoric, and theoretical juridical concepts. Rui Barbosa and Fernando de Azevedo, two prominent Latin American men of letters, are among those who have lamented this condition and the selective myopia it has produced among the educated elite. The disregard for the social sciences, among other disciplines, has long been evident in the scarcity of university courses in the field, and of professional positions available. Demography is no exception to this state of affairs. Still, the situation is improving. Local demographers are receiving training in a couple of regional centers, and the quality of their published output testifies to the rigor of the curriculum. CELADE regularly publishes a journal with high professional standards, in addition to its population index. Today censuses are held with some regularity in most South American countries, and the region's record in this respect is the best in the developing world. Generally, the accuracy of the data has improved, with some notable setbacks. The disparity in the statistical development of individual countries continues to be a problem, but international assistance will eventually

---

[5]Giorgio Mortara, "Appraisal of Census Data for Latin America," *Milbank Memorial Fund Quarterly*, v. 42, no. 2, part 2 (1964): 60.

bring about greater uniformity. Other areas of hoped-for improvement include the increased utilization of census data by national governments, better analysis of data, and speedier and more complete publication of census results.

The Documents. The issues and problems presented above are seen in the references that make up this bibliography. Similarly, the development of demography, more specifically census-taking, in South America is reflected in the uneven distribution of published output and in the shifting subject matter covered. At first glance the most striking fact is simply the difference in the number of works published, both within individual countries at different points in their history, and from country to country. In large measure the relative paucity or abundance of publications in a country is a function of the state of statistics there and of the level of government support for a statistical agency and its activities. Bolivia and Paraguay are cases in point. Each has a short census history, and until very recently demographic information was both scanty and of dubious quality. Little was written on population censuses. Official publications tended to consist of tables and figures with limited or no discussion of methodology, objectives, planning, etc., much less any real evaluation of the quality of the data. Articles by individuals provide some historical background and some analytical discussion. In Brazil the official statistical institute has produced a wealth of publications from early in the century, and some of the credit for this undoubtedly belongs to its sometime director, G. Mortara, whose own output was considerable. Under his guidance the agency produced not only much information on the censuses themselves but also subjected the data to analysis and evaluation. Argentina, despite its somewhat uneven national census record, took numerous early local censuses, provincial as well as municipal. These are frequently very well documented, with lengthy discussions of operational matters, analysis of data, etc. Local support for statistical activities can be seen in the fact that as early as 1852 the state of Buenos Aires had a statistical office which from 1854 on regularly published a journal. Political events can have a clear effect on published output, as they have had in Chile. Following the 1973 coup this country's statistical agency has produced few census publications, and much of the work by individuals is either by foreigners or by Chileans living abroad.

Generally speaking, however, for most countries the number of publications on demographic topics has increased over the past two decades. Regular census taking is no doubt a factor, as censuses tend to provide an impetus for such writings and discussion. The presence of homegrown professional demographers closely involved in census-related activities is another element. This professionalization, as reflected in the writings of individuals, has been a recent and gradual development. Earlier in this century and before, generalists and perhaps historians accounted for most of the non-official works produced. Social scientists then entered the field, and today there is a core of locally trained regional professionals whose productivity is demonstrated by the bibliography at hand. This evolution is evident in the shifting concerns of the works, from an abundance of geographic and historical detail so common in the previous century to a concern with theory, methodology, and evaluation. Automation in particular is providing fertile ground for methodological research as well as opening up new areas of inquiry. The section listing general works for the last two decades shows that the trend has been away from a national focus and increasingly toward a regional approach. In a short time Latin American demographers have become respected members of the international statistical community. Rigorously trained and with a viewpoint shaped by conditions unique to their region, they can be expected to make a genuine contribution to their field.

Bibliography

General Sources

1930-1939

1. James, Preston E. "The Distribution of People in South America." In: Charles C. Colby, ed. *Geographic Aspects of International Relations*. Chicago: University of Chicago Press, 1938. Pp. 215-240.

    Includes methodological notes on mapping and the validity of the census data.

1940-1949

2. Inter-American Statistical Institute. *Bibliography of Selected Statistical Sources of the American Nations*. Washington, D.C.: Pan American Union, 1947.

    An annotated bibliography of the principal statistical materials of the American nations, including data, analyses, methodology, and laws. For each country there is a section on censuses.

3. _____. *Statistical Activities of the American Nations, 1940*. Washington, D.C.: Pan American Union, 1941.

    Compendium of the statistical services and activities of the American nations, together with information concerning statistical personnel. Includes information on population censuses. Continued by separate publications on the statistical activies of individual countries.

4. Library of Congress. Census Library Project. *General Censuses and Vital Statistics in the Americas*. Washington, D.C.: Government Printing Office, 1943.

    An annotated bibliography of the historical censuses of the American republics. Arranged by country.

5. Loyo González, Gilberto. "Bases mínimas para la uniformidad de los censos nacionales de población en el continente americano." Eighth American Scientific Congress, *Proceedings*, v. 8 (1942), pp. 49-51.

    Paper by the director of the Mexican Census Commission.

6. Luna Vegas, Ricardo. "Breve historia de los censos nacionales de población en el hemisferio occidental." *Historia* (April-June 1945), pp. 229-351. Lima.

7. _____. "Métodos de los censos de población de las naciones americanas." *Estadística*, no. 9 (March 1945), pp. 7-133.

A detailed study prepared for the Inter-American Statistical Institute giving background material essential for the development of minimum standards for the proposed hemispheral Census of the Americas in 1950. (See item 8.)

8.   Mendive, Pedro. *Censo de las Américas de 1950: antecedentes y justificación.* Montevideo, 1946.

      Memorandum sent to the Inter-American Statistical Institute by the Inter-American Council of Commerce and Production. It is a critical analysis of Ricardo Luna Vegas' study "Métodos de los censos de poblacón de las naciones americanas" (item 7) with suggestions regarding the projected 1950 Census of the Americas.

9.   United States. Office of Inter-American Affairs. *Populations of the Other American Republics by Major Civil Divisions and by Cities of 5,000 or More Inhabitants. (Handbook of Population Data.)* Washington, D.C., 1945.

      For each country there is a brief discussion of its censuses.

1950-1959

10.   Batschelet, Clarence E.; Archer, Alford. "Comentarios sobre geografía y cartografía para propósitos censales con énfasis en la preparación de mapas para los censos de América de 1960." *Estadística,* v. 16 (March 1958), pp. 29-47.

      Discussion of general purposes and of specific cartographic tasks before and after the enumeration.

11.   Centro Latinoamericano de Demografía. *La evaluación de los resultados de los censos de población levantados en América Latina entre 1947 y 1952.* Santiago, November 1959. (Mimeo.)

12.   _____. *Main Problems Relating to the Organization and Implementation of Programs for the Evaluation, Analysis, and Utilization of Population Census Data in Latin America.* Santiago, December 1959. (Mimeo.)

13.   Inter-American Statistical Institute. "Censos de las naciones americanas: alcance de los programas e informaciones especiales sobre los resultados de los censos de población (incluso analfabetismo) y agropecuario." *Estadística,* v. 14 (September 1956), pp. 485-502.

      Analysis of coverage by country. Includes lists of principal sources.

14.   _____. *Census of Population: Preliminary Results of Further Studies on Some Specific Topics.* Washington, D.C.: Pan American Union, 1956.

15. _____. *Occupational Classification for the 1960 Census of America (COTA-1960)*. Washington, D.C.: Pan American Union, 1959.

16. _____. *The Story of the 1950 Census of the Americas: An Account Prepared in Cooperation with the General Bureaus of Statistics and the National Census Offices of the American Nations*. Washington, D.C.: Pan American Union, 1953.

17. United Nations Statistical Office. *Report of the Regional Census Training Centre for Latin America: Lima, Peru, 11 August to 21 November, 1958*. New York, 1959.

1960-1969

18. Centro Latinoamericano de Demografía. *Censos de población en América Latina; exámen crítica y sugerencias*. Santiago, 1967.
     An evaluation of Latin American population censuses.

19. _____. *Summary of Publications of the Population Census of 15 Latin American Countries around 1950*. Santiago, 1963. (Mimeo.)

20. Inter-American Statistical Institute. *Censo de población: estudios sobre métodos y procedimientos. Programa del Censo de América de 1960 (COTA-1960)*. Washington, D.C.: Pan American Union, 1960.

21. "Programa del Censo de América de 1970 (COTA-1970). Censo de población: proyecto de normas." Presented at the ninth session of the Committee on Improvement of National Statistics, Caracas, Venezuela, August 1967.

22. "Report on the VII Session of the Committee on Improvement of National Statistics. Mexico City, November 28 - December 9, 1960." *Estadística*, v. 18, no. 69, supplement 2 (December 1960).
     Report concerning the 1960 Census of the Americas.

23. Lopes, Valdecir Freire. *La elaboración mecánica en los censos generales*. Inter-American Statistical Institute. Washington, D.C.: Pan American Union, 1960.

24. Miró, Carmen. *Algunos problemas relativos a la evolución de los resultados de los censos de población*. Santiago: Centro Latinoamericano de Demografía, 1963.

25. _____. *La población de America Latina en el siglo XX*. Santiago: Centro Latinoamericano de Demografía, 1965.

26.   Montenegro, Tulio Hostilio. "Bibliografía anotada de las principales fuentes de estadísticas sobre América Latina." *Handbook of Latin American Studies*, no. 29 (1967).

      Bibliography by the Secretary General of the Inter-American Statistical Institute, concerned mainly with post-World War II period. Organized by country.

27.   Mortara, Giorgio. "Appraisal of Census Data for Latin America." *Milbank Memorial Fund Quarterly*, v. 42, no. 2, part 2 (April 1964), pp. 57-85.

      A valuable analysis of the reliability and accuracy (or lack thereof) of Latin American population censuses taken between 1945 and 1954. Panel members' comments on the paper follow.

28.   Stycos, J. Mayone. "Demography and the Study of Population Problems in Latin America." In: Pan-American Assembly on Population. *Population Dilemma in Latin America*. Washington, D.C.: Potomac Books, 1966. Pp. 228-244.

      Laments Latin America's relatively poor demographic statistics and the scarcity of trained demographers. Touches on censuses.

29.   United Nations Technical Assistance Administration. *Seminar on Evaluation and Utilization of Population Census Data in Latin America (Santiago, Chile, 30 November - 18 December, 1959)*. New York, 1960.

      A seminar arranged in order to help Latin American countries utilize the results of the censuses to be held around 1960, as an aid to planning and policy-making. Includes a methodological discussion of procedures such as sampling.

1970-1979

30.   Centro Latinoamericano de Demografía. *Boletín del Banco de Datos*, no. 6 (November 1974). Santiago.

      A publication designed to present the contents of the CELADE data bank. Among the contents: 1960 census data from 16 Latin American countries; 1970 data from 11 countries; statistics on the family (especially from Chile and Brazil); the organization of the data bank; etc.

31.   Herrera Malpica, Nestor; Isea Leonardi, Pedro. "Los censos de población de 1980." *Estadística Venezolana*, no. 6 (January 1976), pp. 59-72.

      The merits of *de jure* and *de facto* population counts, and their use in the 1980 census in Latin America.

32.   Inter-American Statistical Institute. "Composición de disposiciones legales." *Estadística*, v. 33, no. 121 (December 1979), pp. 215-227.

Legislation pertaining to the 1980 census program in Bolivia, Guatemala, Panama, and Venezuela.

33. _____. *Programa del Censo de América de 1970 (COTA-1970). Censos de población: temas, definiciones, clasificaciones y cuestionarios utilizados por los países de la región americana.* Washington, D.C.: Organization of American States, 1977.

34. _____; Brazil. Fundação Instituto Brasileiro de Geografia e Estatística. *Proyecto de normas para los censos de población y habitación del Programa del Censo de América de 1980 (COTA-1980); addendum con observaciones formuladas por Brasil.* Washington, D.C., 1977.

35. Lopes, Valdecir Freire. "Los censos como fuentes de datos demográficos en América Latina." *Notas de Población*, v. 2, no. 5 (August 1974), pp. 49-62.
    Discussion of the recent advances and deficiencies in census-taking in Latin America.

36. _____. "Las fuentes tradicionales de datos demográficos en América Latina." *Notas de Población*, v. 1, no. 2 (August 1973), pp. 17-22.
    Analyzes Latin American censuses during this century and lists the deficiencies in the data. Also mentions recent advances, and the introduction of new procedures such as sampling and test censuses.

37. Mayer, Enrique; Masferrer, Elio. "La población indígena de América en 1978." *América Indígena*, v. 39, no. 2 (April-June 1979), pp. 217-337.
    Discusses the problems of using national censuses for estimating indigenous populations; criteria for defining Indian ethnicity; special "indigenous censuses" carried out by several countries and the quality of the census data obtained.

38. O'Brien, Donald J. "Census Data in Latin America: Considerations for the Research Specialist." In: Robert N. Thomas, ed. *Population Dynamics of Latin America: A Review and Bibliography.* Papers presented at the Second General Session of the Conference of Latin Americanist Geographers, Boston, April 17, 1971. East Lansing, Mich.: Clag Publications, 1973. Pp. 1-24.
    A summary of the state of Latin America's censuses in 1971, with a brief history and commentary.

39. Pantelides, Edith A. "El hogar como unidad de análisis de los datos censales: importancia y posibilidades." In: Centro Latinoamericano de Demografía. *La familia como unidad de estudio demográfico.* San José, Costa Rica, 1976.

40. Rivas González, Ernesto; Isea Leonardi, Pedro. "Algunos problemas de los censos de
     población en América Latina." *Estadística Venezolana*, no. 8 (October 1976), pp. 115-
     132.
          Authors discuss problems in the different phases of the 1973 census round
     and future Latin American censuses in the context of the rapid population growth in
     the region.

41. Sánchez-Albornoz, Nicolás. *The Population of Latin America: A History*. Berkeley and Los
     Angeles: University of California Press, 1974.
          A demographic history of Latin America. Censuses are discussed throughout.
     Good bibliography.

42. Somoza, Jorge L. "Una idea para estimar la población emigrante por sexo y edad en el
     censo de un país." *Notas de Población*, v. 5, no. 15 (December 1977), pp. 89-106.
          Puts forward a method for estimating the number of emigrants from a country,
     using as basis census information on Latin American migrants living in countries
     other than their own.

43. Stockwell, Edward G.; Wicks, Jerry W. "Digit Preference and Avoidance in Some Recent
     Latin American Censuses." *Estadística*, v. 28, no. 108 (September 1970), pp. 380-
     383.

44. Torrado, Susana. "Algunas reflexiones sobre los censos de 1980, relacionadas con la
     investigación sociodemográfica y las políticas de población en la América Latina."
     Notas de Población, v. 5, no. 14 (August 1977), pp. 109-148.
          The author discusses problems encountered by socio-demographic investigators
     in dealing with Latin American census data. Suggestions are presented for inclusion
     in the 1980 census.

45. United Nations. Economic Commission for Latin America. *La experiencia
     latinoamericana en los censos de población de 1970 y orientaciones para los censos de
     1980*. Santiago, 1978.
          Deals with census organization and administration and the processing of cen-
     sus data, and analyzes the results.

46. _____. *Informe sobre conclusiones*. Santiago, 1979.
          Report on a seminar held in 1978 to evaluate Latin American censuses. Discus-
     sion focuses on census methodology, design, and organization, and recommenda-
     tions for improvements are made.

47. _____. *Report of the Seminar on the Preparation and Use of Population and Housing Cen-
     sus Tabulations*. Santiago, 1973.

1980-1989

48.   Argentina, Government of; Mexico, Government of. *Propuesta de programa regional de censos de población y vivienda presentada por las delegaciones de Argentina y México.* Washington, D.C.: Organization of American States, 1986.

A proposal for an inter-American regional census plan for the 1990s, put forward at the 1986 Inter-American Statistical Conference. Covers financing and technological assistance as well as major methodological issues.

49.   Argentina. Instituto Nacional de Estadística y Censos. *Seminario regional sobre características económicas de la población en los censos del 90: informe.* Buenos Aires, [1986].

Report concludes that the 1980 census round failed to measure certain economic characteristics in the population. Recommendations are made to revise the questionnaires used.

50.   _____; Centro Latinoamericano de Demografía; Canadian International Development Agency. *Los censos de población del 80: taller de análisis y evaluación.* Buenos Aires: Instituto Nacional de Estadística y Censos, 1985.

Proceedings from a 1985 workshop on developments in census-taking, especially in relation to the 1980 Latin American censuses. The use of samples, census cartography, contents of census form, data processing, etc.

51.   Arretx, Carmen; Chackiel, Juan. "Algunos problemas relativos a la recolección de datos demográficos en los censos de población de América Latina en la década de 1980." *Notas de Población*, v. 14, no. 42 (December 1986), pp. 51-76.

Description of methods of data collecting in the 1980 census round in Latin America.

52.   Goyer, Doreen S.; Domschke, Eliane. *The Handbook of National Population Censuses. Latin America and the Caribbean, North America, and Oceania.* Westport, Conn.: Greenwood Press, 1983.

For each country presents a history of census-taking, including evaluation of quality. For post-1945 period each census is discussed in some detail, including its concepts and definitions, special elements and features, quality, publication plan for data. Names official statistical agencies and government statistical publications. An important source.

53.   Lopes, Valdecir Freire. "Los censos de población y vivienda: críticas y sugerencias." *Notas de Población*, v. 9, no. 25 (April 1981), pp. 69-92.

Latin American censuses are evaluated for their advantages and limitations as sources of demographic data, as determined by their methodological characteristics.

Problems in census data gathering are mentioned, and suggestions are made to improve the utilization of the data.

54.   Moreira, Maxwell Ribeiro. *América Latina: evaluación y corrección de la preferencia de digitos en la declaración de la edad: trabajo final de investigación*. Santiago: Centro Latinoamericano de Demografía, 1985. (Mimeo.)
         Demonstrates the application of different statistical techniques to evaluate and correct error in declaration of age, utilizing data of high, medium, and low quality from three Latin American countries.

55.   Packer, Abel. "Aspectos relevantes de la organización de servicios de procesamiento electrónico de datos de censos y encuestas en América Latina." *Notas de Población*, v. 8, no. 24 (December 1980), pp. 45-56.
         Stresses the need for Latin American national statistical agencies to make use of recent advances in the field of electronic data processing, and lists the requirements to reach this objective: the hiring of qualified personnel, increased use of specialized software and systems, cooperation with other institutions to exchange experiences, etc.

56.   Silva, Ari N. *Experiencia en el procesamiento de los censos en América Latina en la década del 80*. Buenos Aires: Instituto Nacional de Estadística y Censos, 1985.
         Examines the experiences of the Centro Latinoamericano de Demografía in processing some recent Latin American censuses, and provides a detailed listing of the various stages of the censuses and the specific tasks associated with each.

57.   _____. "Procesamiento de los censos de población de América Latina en la década de 1990: un vistazo al futuro." *Notas de Población*, v. 14, no. 41 (August 1986), pp. 9-24.
         Analyzes data processing methods to be used in upcoming Latin American population censuses.

58.   Torrado, Susana. "Los censos de población y vivienda de América Latina durante el período 1970-1980: recomendaciones y prácticas." In: Susana Torrado, ed. *Investigación e información sociodemográficas 2*. Série Población. Buenos Aires: Consejo Latinoamericano de Ciencias Sociales, 1981. Pp. 3-60.
         Detailed discussion of the information requested in Latin American censuses during the 1970s. Although mainly descriptive, the study also points out deficiencies and makes recommendations.

59.   _____. "La familia como unidad de análisis en censos de población y vivienda." In: Susana Torrado, ed. *La familia como unidad de análisis en censos y encuestas de*

hogares: metodología actual y prospectiva en América Latina. Buenos Aires: Centro de Estudios Urbanos y Regionales, 1983. Pp. 199-277.

Critically examines the methodology currently in use, to discover its strengths and weaknesses and to propose alternative procedures in order to improve the quality and quantity of the information obtained in population censuses.

60. _____; Zúñiga, Luís. "Los censos de población y vivienda en la década de 1980 en América Latina. Tercera reunión del grupo de trabajo sobre información socio-demográfica (Lima, 21-25 de mayo de 1979). Relatorio de los debates." In: Susana Torrado, ed. *Investigación e información sociodemográficas 2.* Série Población. Buenos Aires: Consejo Latinoamericano de Ciencias Sociales, 1981. Pp. 251-274.

The proceedings of a working group discussing the conceptual contents of Latin American censuses in the 1970s.

61. United Nations. Economic Commission for Latin America. *Boletín de actividades de censos de población y habitación,* nos. 6 - . Santiago, 1980- .

A report on the progress of preparations for the 1980 census round in Latin America.

Argentina

1880-1889

62. Buenos Aires (City). *Censo general de población, edificación, comercio e industrias de la ciudad de Buenos Aires. Levantado en los días 17 de agosto, 15 y 30 de setiembre de 1887.* Buenos Aires: Compañía Sud-Americana de Billetes de Banco, 1889.

Contains a brief discussion of methodology, and a chapter on the demographic history of Buenos Aires, including descriptions and evaluations of previous censuses. Vol. 2 has a detailed analysis of data obtained in 1887 census.

63. Buenos Aires (Province). *Censo general de la provincia de Buenos Aires, demográfico, agrícola, industrial, comercial, etc., verificado el 9 de octubre de 1881.* Buenos Aires: Imprenta de El Diario, 1883.

Brief description and analysis of the 1881 census.

1890-1899

64.   Argentina. Comisión Directiva del Censo. *Segundo censo de la República Argentina, mayo 10 de 1895*. Buenos Aires: Taller Tipográfico de la Penitenciaría Nacional, 1898.
       Introduction discusses objectives, plan, execution, personnel, some methodology. Vol. 2 has very detailed analysis of the data obtained.

1900-1909

65.   Buenos Aires (City). *Censo general de población, edificación, comercio e industrias de la ciudad de Buenos Aires. Levantado en los días 11 y 18 de septiembre de 1904*. Buenos Aires: Compañía Sud-Americana de Billetes de Banco, 1906.
       Contains a discussion of methodology, including statistical procedures. Presents sample questionnaire, with a list of instructions for filling it out. Analyzes results of census. Good source.

66.   _____. *Estudio del censo arjentino de 1895*. Santiago: Imprenta Litografía i Encuadernación Barcelona, 1904.
       Detailed study of the practical aspects of the 1895 Argentinean census, including census questions, personnel, methodology. Its purpose: to use the census as a model for Chile. Valuable source.

67.   Rosario (City). *Primer censo municipal de población con datos sobre edificación, comercio e industria de la ciudad del Rosario de Santa Fe, . . . levantado el día 19 de octubre de 1900*. Buenos Aires: Litografía, Imprenta y Encuadernación de Guillermo Kraft, 1902.
       Brief discussion of census.

68.   _____. *Segundo censo municipal de la ciudad del Rosario de Santa Fe, . . . levantado el 19 de octubre de 1906*. Rosario: Tipografía, Litografía y Encuadernación La Capital, 1908.
       Description and analysis of municipal census.

1910-1919

69.   Argentina. Comisión Nacional del Censo. *Tercer censo nacional, levantado el 1 de junio de 1914*. Buenos Aires: Talleres Gráficos de L.J. Rosso, 1916.
       Vol. 1 contains a very detailed description of the 1914 census: plan, execution, all practical aspects and procedures, methodology. Includes analysis of the results. A valuable source.

70. Buenos Aires (City). *Censo general de población, edificación, comercio e industrias de la ciudad de Buenos Aires*. Buenos Aires: Compañía Sud-Americana de Billetes de Banco, 1910.

    Introduction contains plan, mode of execution, comparison with previous censuses, tabulation of the present census, methodology, statistical procedures used, maps, analysis of results, and an extensive discussion of each census concept used in the questionnaire. Important source. Also published in French.

1930-1939

71. Ardissone, Romualdo. "La ciudad de Buenos Aires excede los límites de la Capital Federal. Necesidad de levantar un censo que abarque la totalidad de la aglomeración urbana bonaerense." *Anales de la Sociedad Argentina de Estudios Geográficos*, v. 5 (1937), pp. 467-471.

72. Besio Moreno, Nicolás. *Buenos Aires. Puerto del Río de La Plata, capital de la Argentina. Estudio crítico de su población 1536-1936*. Buenos Aires, 1939.

    An important source, especially the chapter entitled: "Historia de los censos de Buenos Aires, 1536-1936," pp. 305-352. Lists and discusses every major and minor census in Buenos Aires within the stated period, with some evaluations.

73. Buenos Aires (City). *Cuarto censo general, 1936. Población. 22-X-1936*. Buenos Aires, 1938.

    Vol. 1 consists mainly of a very detailed description of all the practical aspects of the census, real and anticipated problems, methodology, census personnel, etc. A very valuable source.

74. Dieulefait, Carlos E. *Estadística censal y estadística administrativas argentinas*. Rosario: Talleres Gráficos Pomponio, 1935.

1940-1949

75. Argentina. Dirección General del Servicio Estadístico Nacional. *IV censo general de la nación*. Buenos Aires, [n.d.].

    1947 census. Vol. 1 describes in detail methodology and the processing of the data obtained. Followed by statement of objectives, a general discussion of the census, and an analysis of the results. A valuable source.

76. _____. *IV censo general de la nación. Cuestionarios censales, planillas y formularios impresos*. Buenos Aires, 1947.

Includes an explanatory resumé, and samples of the schedules for the various censuses.

77.   Besio Moreno, Nicolás. "Rosario de Santa Fe, cartografía y población, 1744-1942." *Revista del Museo de La Plata*, Sección Geología, n.s., v. 1 (1943), pp. 259-298.

Detailed study of the demographic history of Rosario, including systematic coverage of all local, provincial, and national censuses.

78.   Buenos Aires, Universidad de. Instituto de Sociología. "El Instituto de Sociología y el cuarto censo nacional." *Boletín del Instituto de Sociología*, v. 4 (1945), pp. 133-136.

Report includes a list of the questions suggested for the census schedules.

79.   Dagnino Pastore, Lorenzo. "Comparaciones y correcciones demográficas determinadas por el cuarto censo general de la nación." *Revista de la Facultad de Ciencias Económicas*, v. 1, no. 1 (1948), pp. 21-46. Buenos Aires.

Trends in population growth in Argentina, 1864-1947, with revisions of estimates based on the last census.

80.   Instituto Alejandro E. Bunge de Investigaciones Económicas y Sociales. "Acerca de los resultados del IV censo nacional." *Revista de Economía Argentina*, v. 47, no. 349 (July 1947), pp. 192-198; v. 47, no. 351 (September 1947), pp. 264-266; v. 47, no. 352 (October 1947), pp. 207-310; v. 47, no. 354 (December 1947), pp. 380-383.

Results of the fourth national census. The December issue discusses the difference between the population size shown in the May 1947 census and the estimate made earlier based on the 1914 census, and the reasons for the difference.

81.   Inter-American Statistical Institute. *Las actividades estadísticas de las naciones americanas. Argentina.* Washington, D.C.: Pan American Union, 1941.

82.   Llorens, Emilio. "Los resultados del reciente censo y los cálculos de Alejandro E. Bunge." *Revista de Economía Argentina*, v. 47, no. 350 (August 1947), pp. 223-225.

A comparison of the results of the 1947 census figures for the total population of Argentina with the estimates made by the Instituto Alejandro E. Bunge (see item 80), and reasons for the difference.

83.   Mendoza (Province). Ministerio de Economía, Obras Públicas y Riego. *Memoria correspondiente a los años 1938 a 1941 presentada a la H. Legislatura 18 de febrero 1938-1941.* V. II. Mendoza: Best, 1943.

The section "Censo general de la población . . .", pp. 43-54, includes the message to the legislature recommending the census, and the law itself. There is also a brief history of the actual and projected censuses of the province.

84.   Monteagudo, Emilio. "Acerca del censo general." *Revista de Economía Argentina*, v. 43, no. 305 (November 1943).

85.   Vaccaro, Juan M. "El próximo censo general de la nación." *Revista de Ciencias Económicas*, ser. 2, v. 30, no. 248 (March 1942), pp. 213-222.
       Stresses the importance of the general census of 1950.

1950-1959

86.   Argentina. Dirección General del Servicio Estadístico Nacional. *IV censo general de la nación. 1947. Comparación de los resultados del censo de población.* Buenos Aires, 1951.
       Brief account of earlier censuses in Argentina. Compares 1947 data with those of 1869, 1895, and 1914 censuses for various population categories and analyzes the results of the comparison.

1960-1969

87.   Argentina. Consejo Federal de Inversiones. Biblioteca. *Bibliografía: Los censos argentinos por regiones.* Buenos Aires, 1968.
       Extensively annotated bibliography of national, provincial, municipal, and private censuses taken in Argentina between 1869 and 1960. Introduction gives a brief overview of the history of census-taking in the country from 1809. Contents of census publications is described volume by volume. A very important source.

88.   Camisa, Zulma C. *Argentina: Evaluación y ajuste del censo de población de 1960, por sexo y edad, y tabla abreviada de mortalidad, 1959-1961.* Santiago: Centro Latinoamericano de Demografía, 1964.

89.   Cataldi, Alberto. *Algunos análisis de las cifras provisionales del censo de población de Argentina de 1960, con especial referencia a la provincia de Buenos Aires.* Santiago: Centro Latinoamericano de Demografía, 1961. (Mimeo.)

90.   Cerisola, M. J. Elsa. *Proyección quinquenal de la población, 1965-2000. Incluye la estimación de omisión diferencial por origen, sexo y grupos de edad de la población censada al 30 de setiembre de 1960.* Buenos Aires: Instituto Nacional de Estadística y Censos, 1968.

91.   Cirigliano, Antonio. "Población extranjera según su origen y radicación geográfica (censos 1895, 1914 y 1947)." *Revista de la Dirección Nacional de Migraciones*, no. 3 (1960).

92.   Dehollain, Alejandro; Salvia, F.; Somoza, Jorge L. "Examen crítico de algunas estadísticas de población de la Argentina." *Desarrollo Económico*, v. 2, no. 2 (July-September 1962). Buenos Aires.

93.   Keyfitz, Nathan. "The Argentine Census of September 30, 1960." *Estadística*, v. 18 (December 1960), pp. 647-654.

94.   Lattes, Alfredo E. *Evaluación y ajuste de algunos resultados de los tres primeros censos de población*. Buenos Aires: Instituto Torcuato di Tella, Centro de Investigaciones Sociales, 1968.

95.   _____; Poczter, R. *Muestra del censo de población de la ciudad de Buenos Aires de 1855*. Buenos Aires, 1968.

96.   Maeder, Ernesto J. A. "El censo de población de 1857 para la Confederación Argentina." *Revista de la Junta de Historia de Corrientes*, no. 1 (1966), pp. 93-128.
      Detailed history of the 1857 census and an analysis of its results.

97.   _____. "Demografía y potencial humano de Corrientes. El censo provincial de 1814." *Nordeste*, no. 5 (1963). Resistencia.

98.   _____. *Evolución demográfica argentina desde 1810 a 1869*. Buenos Aires: Editorial Universitaria, 1969.
      Lists and describes, with some evaluation, all national and regional censuses in Argentina within the stated time frame, as part of the discussion of the larger theme. This is followed by an analysis and comparison of the census data (along with other population data). Extensive footnotes list primary historical sources. An important historical study.

99.   _____. "Historia y resultados del censo confederal de 1857." *Trabajos y Comunicaciones*, no. 18 (1968). La Plata.

100. Misiones (Province). Dirección General de Estadística. *Evaluación de la integridad del censo de la población de 1960 en Misiones*. Publication no. 1. Posadas: Sección Técnica, 1968.
      Evaluates the completeness of the 1960 census in Misiones.

101. Somoza, Jorge L.; Lattes, Alfredo E. *Muestras de los dos primeros censos nacionales de población, 1869 y 1895*. Buenos Aires: Instituto Torcuato di Tella, Centro de Investigaciones Sociales, 1967.
      Presents the methodology for obtaining the samples and verifies the data obtained.

102. Vapñarsky, César A. *La población urbana argentina: revisión crítica del método y los resultados censales de 1960.* Buenos Aires: Centro de Estudios Urbanos y Regionales, 1968.

103. _____. *Población urbana y población metropolitana: criterios para el relevamiento de información censal en la Argentina.* Buenos Aires: Editorial del Instituto Torcuato di Tella, 1969.

1970-1979

104. Argentina. Instituto Nacional de Estadística y Censos. *Censo nacional de población, familias y viviendas, 1970. Resultados obtenidos por muestra. Total del país.* Buenos Aires, 1974.
      Describes 1970 census. Introductory discussion of objectives, basic definitions and concepts, test census, methodology, sampling errors. Sample questionnaire included.

105. _____. *Cuadros inéditos del IV censo general de la nación, año 1947. Características de familia y convivencia, estado civil y fecundidad.* Buenos Aires, 1970.
      Title: "Unpublished tables from the fourth census . . . ." Discusses basic concepts used; census questions; instructions for filling out schedules. Compares methodology and concepts with those of the censuses of 1960 and 1970. Includes sample questionnaire.

106. Canton, Dario; Moreno, José Luís. *Pequeño censo de 1927.* Buenos Aires: Instituto Torcuato di Tella, Centro de Investigaciones Sociales, 1971.
      A "census" for 1927 taken in 1965-1966 by sociologists, utilizing earlier data. Introduction describes methodology and objectives.

107. Griva, Edelmi E. "Síntesis del Censo Indígena Nacional realizado en la República Argentina." *América Indígena,* v. 30, no. 3 (1970), pp. 657-672.
      Describes the 1965-1968 census of the Indian population of Argentina, including methodology and an evaluation.

108. Misiones (Province). Dirección General de Estadística y Censos. *Censo integral del área de frontera, 1978.* Posadas, Misiones, 1978.
      A number of publications on methodology and organization are available: a tabulation plan, instructions for the various department heads, an enumerator's manual, schedules, a personnel chart.

109. _____. *Censo integral del área de frontera, 1978: resultados generales.* Posadas, Misiones, 1979.

In addition to the census results there is a section on organization and ad-ministration, personnel, and data collection and processing. Appendix contains enumerator's manual and sample schedule.

110.   Vapñarsky, César A. *La población urbana argentina en 1970 y 1960: revisión crítica de la información censal oficial.* Buenos Aires: Centro de Estudios Urbanos y Regionales, 1979.

   Detailed critique of definitions and procedures used in the 1960 and 1970 cen-suses in Argentina to determine the size of urban areas. Reinterpretation of census figures.

111.   Viglione de Arrastia, Hebe. *Censos de la Provincia de Santa Fe; bibliografía cronológica y comentada.* Santa Fe: Instituto Provincial de Estadística y Censos, 1976.

   Part I consists of a chronological list of censuses; Part II is a commentated bibli-ography of the same censuses.

1980-1989

112.   Argentina. Instituto Nacional de Estadística y Censos. *Censo nacional de población y vivienda 1980.* Buenos Aires, 1980.

   In nine separate documents, some of the materials used in the 1980 census: in-structions to administrators and enumerators, schedules, and other forms.

113.   _____. *Censo nacional de población y vivienda 1980. Serie B. Características generales. Total del país.* Buenos Aires, 1981.

   Series B comprises 27 volumes, one for each region. The volume for the country as a whole contains information on the operational and methodological aspects of the census, and an evaluation of the census quality. There is also a section on the demographic history of Argentina.

114.   _____. *Censo nacional de población y vivienda 1980. Serie D. Población. Total del país.* Buenos Aires, 1980.

   Series D contains the final population results for the whole country. There is also a demographic history of Argentina, and a detailed discussion of methodology and of the statistical procedures and concepts used, such as standard error and the use of representative samples.

115.   _____. *Diseño de la muestra del censo nacional de población y vivienda 1980.* Buenos Aires, 1986.

   Discussion of the use of sampling in the 1980 census, with an evaluation of its procedures and implementation. Some of the results are analyzed.

116. Bernacchi, Margarita; González Villalobos, Alvaro; Novaro de Cosarinsky, Sara; et al. "Diseño de la muestra del censo nacional de población y vivienda de 1980— Argentina: procedimientos de selección, estimación, etc." *Estadística. Avance*, v. 37, no. 1 (July 1985), pp. 1-32.

Discusses aspects of the first occasion of sampling being used in an Argentinean census: the design of the sample, procedures for selection and estimation, sampling error, etc.

117. Boleda, Mario. *Censos de población para la provincia de Salta, 1947-1980.* Salta: Grupo de Estudios Socio-Demográficos, 1987.

Analysis and critical evaluation of census data from the province of Salta.

118. Cortés, Rosalia. *Actividad económica oculta entre los inactivos del censo de 1980: algunas propuestas para su medición en el censo de 1990.* Buenos Aires: Centro de Estudios de Población, 1986.

Discusses how to improve the measurement of underemployment in the 1990 census, by analyzing the 1980 data for the economically active population.

119. Elizalde, María Laura. *Desafío para el censo de 1990: qué hacer con las ocupaciones?* Buenos Aires: Centro de Estudios de Población, 1986.

The problems of definition and codification of the classification of occupations.

120. Fernández Pernas, José. "Lectura automática de los cuestionarios censales en el censo de población y vivienda de 1980 en Argentina." In: Argentina. Instituto Nacional de Estadística y Censos; United Nations. Economic Commission for Latin America; Centro Latinoamericano de Demografía. *Censos de población del 80: taller de análisis y evaluación.* Buenos Aires: Instituto Nacional de Estadística y Censos, 1985. Pp. 359-362.

Description of the implementation of automatic reading of census questionnaires in Argentina, beginning with a test census.

121. García, María Nieves. *Comparabilidad de la información económica en los censos de población.* Buenos Aires: Centro de Estudios de Población, 1986.

A study of the 1960, 1970, and 1980 census data on economic information to determine their comparability.

122. González Villalobos, Alvaro. "Sobre algunos aspectos de la aplicación de métodos estadísticos de muestreo en el censo de población de 1980 en la Argentina." In: Argentina. Instituto Nacional de Estadística y Censos; United Nations. Economic Commission for Latin America; Centro Latinoamericano de Demografía. *Censos de población del 80: taller de análisis y evaluación.* Buenos Aires: Instituto Nacional de Estadística y Censos, 1985. Pp. 319-325.

A discussion of the first-time use of sampling in an Argentine census: objectives, design, selection, results, evaluation, errors.

123.   Kritz, Ernesto H. *Posibilidad de medición de la subutilización de la fuerza de trabajo a través de los censos de población*. Buenos Aires: Centro de Estudios de Población, 1986.
Suggests using a much more extensive questionnaire for a sample of the population in order to measure the informal economy.

124.   Lindenboim, Javier. *Problema de las "actividades no bien especificadas" en la clasificación por rama de la población económicamente activa*. Buenos Aires: Centro de Estudios de Población, 1986.
Discussion of the concern that the category "Unspecified" in the list of occupations is too broad.

125.   Minujin, Alberto. *Acerca de los censos del 90*. Buenos Aires: Centro de Estudios de Población, 1986.
A survey of Argentinean censuses since 1869, comparing their themes, questions, questionnaires, and publications.

126.   Orsatti, Alvaro. *Proyecciones de población: evaluación a partir del censo de 1980*. Buenos Aires: Centro Interamericano para el Desarrollo Social, 1982.
Evaluation of population projections by the national statistical office, based on a comparison with the 1980 census figures.

127.   Pantelides, Edith A. *Análisis y propuesta de corrección de la información sobre estado civil en los cuatro primeros censos nacionales argentinos*. Buenos Aires: Centro de Estudios de Población, 1984.
Brief but important source. Evaluation and proposed correction for one population category in the first four censuses.

128.   Somoza, Jorge L. *Censo experimental de Junín de los Andes: resultados y análisis*. Santiago: Centro Latinoamericano de Demografía, 1987.
Experimental census to investigate methods of data collection on infant mortality that would yield more reliable results than those obtained in the 1970 and 1980 national population censuses.

129.   _____. "Cobertura del censo de 1980 en comparación con la de los censos de 1960 y 1970." In: Argentina. Instituto Nacional de Estadística y Censos; United Nations. Economic Commission for Latin America; Centro Latinoamericano de Demografía. *Censos de población del 80: taller de análisis y evaluación*. Buenos Aires: Instituto Nacional de Estadística y Censos, 1985. Pp. 102-103.

A comparison of the coverage of the last three Argentinean censuses. Concludes that the last census achieved the best coverage.

130.   Vapñarsky, César A. *Censo de población y vivienda de 1980: comentarios críticos sobre su cartografía y su definición de "localidad"*. Buenos Aires: Instituto Nacional de Estadística y Censos, 1985. (Mimeo.)
       Criticizes the identification and delimitation of "locality" in the 1980 census as being too broad, thereby greatly reducing the value of the census figures for smaller municipalities.

131.   Wainerman, Catalina H.; Moreno, Martín. *Hacia el reconocimiento censal de las mujeres trabajadoras*. Buenos Aires: Centro de Estudios de Población, 1986.
       On the need to measure the number of working women in Argentina by means of census questions.

132.   _____; _____. *Productoras de subsistencia ingresan a las estadísticas censales*. Buenos Aires: Centro de Estudios de Población, 1986.
       Addresses the problem of censuses failing to include the contributions of working women to the economy, especially in developing countries and in the field of agriculture. Details an empirical experiment to rectify this situation, carried out in two localities in Argentina.

133.   _____; _____. *Sensibilizando a los censistas a los sesgos sexuales: un ejercicio de entrenamiento*. Buenos Aires: Centro de Estudios de Población, 1986.
       Discussion of the need to train census personnel in order to reduce sexual stereotyping (e.g. the automatic classification of women as "house-wives").

Bolivia

1900-1909

134.   Bolivia. Dirección Nacional de Estadística. *Censo de 1900: métodos y procedimientos*.
       Materials used in taking the population census of September 10, 1900. Acquired in connection with an Inter-American Statistical Institute survey on census methods taken in 1944. Contents: correspondence, laws and decrees.

135.   Bolivia. Oficina Nacional de Inmigración, Estadística y Propaganda Geográfica. *Censo general de la población de la República de Bolivia según el empadronamiento del 10 de septiembre de 1900*. La Paz: J.M. Gamarra, 1902-1904.
       Describes the 1900 census by regional department, noting quality problems. Includes information on organization and procedures.

1940-1949

136.   Bolivia. Dirección General de Estadística. *Plan para el levantamiento del censo de población de la ciudad de La Paz, 1942*. La Paz, 1942.
       Plan for taking population census of La Paz in 1942.

137.   García Rosquellas, R. *Breve historia de la estadística nacional*. Universidad Mayor de San Francisco Javier, Publicación de la Facultad de Derecho, Ciencias Políticas y Sociales, Estudios Histórico-legales, no. 2. Sucre, 1942.
       Description and critique of the "censuses" of 1869, 1880, and 1900.

138.   Soroco, Carlos. "Análisis del censo de Cochabamba." *Revista Jurídica*, v. 12, no. 48 (June 1949), pp. 29-62.
       Analysis of the Cochabamba census of 1945.

1950-1959

139.   Bolivia. Dirección General de Estadística y Censos. *Censo demográfico 1950*. La Paz: Editorial Argote, 1955.
       Brief introduction, and a chapter on the legal and administrative basis of the census.

140.   Inter-American Statistical Institute. *Actividades estadísticas de las naciones americanas. Bolivia*. Washington, D.C.: Pan American Union, 1959.
       Describes statistical activies in Bolivia, including a section in Spanish and English on censuses. Special attention is given to the 1950 census, describing its organization, tabulation, and publications.

1960-1969

141.   Bolivia. Dirección General de Estadística y Censos. *Informe del Departamento Nacional de Muestreo, el 1 de octubre de 1962 - el 31 de julio de 1963*. La Paz, [1963].
       Contains instructions and questionnaires used in the demographic census by sampling.

1970-1979

142. Averanga Mollinedo, Asthenio. *Aspectos generales de la población boliviana*. La Paz: Librería Editorial "Juventud", 1974.

    Discusses national census of 1950 and subsequent regional censuses, presenting methodology and interpretation of results. Includes data from and brief discussion of earlier censuses, going back to colonial times. Together with Torrez Pinto 1977 (item 149) among the best analytical and historical overviews of Bolivian population censuses, despite its brevity.

143. Bolivia. Instituto Nacional de Estadística. *Censo de población y habitación Tarija*. La Paz, 1970.

    Introduction briefly discusses objectives, definitions, classifications, and categories of census. Gives a few details on methodology, and touches on census administration.

144. _____. *Censo de población y vivienda, Ciudad de Oruro, 23 mayo 1972*. La Paz, 1975.
    See item 143.

145. _____. *Censo de población y vivienda, Ciudad de Potosí, septiembre de 1972*. La Paz, 1974.
    See item 143.

146. _____. *Censo de población y vivienda, Ciudad de Sucre, septiembre 1972*. La Paz, 1975.
    See item 143.

147. _____. *Censo de población y vivienda, 1976*. La Paz, 1976.

    Ten volumes of census agency documents used in the census. Contents: questionnaire, objectives and basic procedures, census organization, instructions for preparing cartographic materials, rules for codification of census districts, a pre-census work manual, etc.

148. _____. *Informe de la comisión para el estudio de la boleta censal*. La Paz, 1976.

    Report on the methodology used in the development of the questionnaire for the 1976 census.

149. Torrez Pinto, Hugo. *Rasgos y consideraciones demográficas de Bolivia*. Centro de Investigaciones Sociales, Serie de Estudios de Población y Desarrollo, no. 15. La Paz: Ediciones C.I.S., 1977.

    Discusses national censuses from 1825 to the present, noting differences in quality and comparability. See item 142.

1980-1989

150.   Bolivia. Instituto Nacional de Estadística. *Boletín Demográfico Departamental*. La Paz, 1980.

   Nine volumes, one for each regional department, analyzing the results of the 1976 national census. Contains little on methodology, with no attempt at evaluation.

151.   _____. *Censos experimentales: una descripción crítica; documento preliminar*. La Paz, 1986.

   Description of the organization of the 1985 test census, and the activities connected with that census. Includes the contents of the questionnaire; the organization of the fieldwork; codification, processing, and evaluation of the data. Documents included.

152.   _____. *Informe del seminario de evaluación del levantamiento del censo nacional de población y vivienda del 29 de septiembre de 1976*. La Paz, 1980.

   Proceedings of a seminar held to evaluate the methodology of the 1976 census. Topics: census mapping, personnel selection and training, subjects investigated, data processing, evaluation of methodology, analysis and publication of results, administrative problems. Summary reports on each phase of the census, sample questionnaires, conclusions reached by the participants in the seminar, etc.

153.   _____. *Proyecto de financiamiento para el censo nacional de población y vivienda 1986 de la República de Bolivia*. La Paz: Ministerio de Planeamiento y Coordinación, 1985.

   Proposal for financing the 1986 Bolivian census.

154.   _____; United Nations. Economic Commission for Latin America; Centro Latinoamericano de Demografía. *Censos experimentales: una descripción crítica*. La Paz: Instituto Nacional de Estadística, 1986.

   A workshop to examine critically the three test censuses taken in Bolivia in 1985 in preparation for the 1988 general census. Emphasizes methodology. Recommendations for improvements are listed.

155.   Cavallini, Carlos. *Evaluación de los censos: aplicación al caso de Bolivia; versión preliminar*. Santiago: Economic Commission for Latin America, 1981. (Mimeo.)

   An evaluation by a U.N. agency of Bolivia's 1976 census. Aims: to demonstrate the utility of census data, to assess the quality of the data, and to help improve future censuses. The methodology of evaluation is extensively covered.

156.   Medica, Vilma. *Análisis de los resultados del censo nacional de población y vivienda de 1976: informe final de los resultados del Proyecto Bol/78/P02*. La Paz [n.p.], 1981.

Report on a project undertaken to assist and improve the quality of statistical activities in Bolivia, based on the 1976 census.

157. Mezza Rosso, Victor. *Situación demográfica de Bolivia: sobre los resultados censales 1976.* La Paz: Instituto Nacional de Estadística, 1980.

Analysis of the results of the 1976 population census, by an official of the national statistical agency.

158. Vidal Z., David E.; Camacho Villarroel, Miriam; Fernández Medrano, Julio; et al. *Evaluación de la encuesta por enumeración completa de la ciudad de Cochabamba 1983.* Cochabamba: Centro de Estudios de Población, 1986.

The quality of a city population survey is examined and the conclusions tested by reference to the census of 1976, using the same methods of evaluation.

Brazil

1920-1929

159. Brazil. Directoria Geral de Estatística. *Instrucções para a apuração do censo demographico.* Rio de Janeiro: Typ. da Estatística, 1921.

160. _____. *Recenseamento do Brasil, realizado em 1 de setembro de 1920.* Rio de Janeiro: Typ. da Estatística, 1922.

Vol. 1 presents a detailed summary of population calculations for Brazil between 1776 and 1869. The Appendix to vol. 1 describes the legal basis for census-taking and presents operational information, compilation of results, methodology. Also contains sample questionnaires.

1930-1939

161. Braga, André Duarte. "O recenseamento de 1940; conferência realizada no 'Curso de informações' de 1939 do IBGE." Rio de Janeiro: Instituto Brasileiro de Geografia e Estatística, 1939.

162. Brazil. Instituto Brasileiro de Geografia e Estatística. *Algumas sugestões para a propaganda do recenseamento de 1940.* Rio de Janeiro, 1939.

Some suggestions concerning publicity for the upcoming 1940 census.

1940-1949

163.   Brazil. Instituto Brasileiro de Geografia e Estatística. *Análises de resultados do censo demográfico.* Rio de Janeiro, 1944-1945.

A collection in six volumes of 240 statistical and demographic studies based on the 1940 census results.

164.   _____. *Aplicações do censo demográfico para a reconstrução e emenda das estatísticas do movimiento da população.* Rio de Janeiro, [1948?].

Use of the population census for the improvement and correction of vital statistics.

165.   _____. *Características demográficas do Estado da Bahia.* Rio de Janeiro, 1949.

One chapter discusses the results of the 1872 census in the State of Bahia.

166.   _____. "Estudos e análises do recenseamento de 1940." *Revista Brasileira de Estatística,* v. 10, no. 38 (April-June 1949), pp. 310-322.

A list of publications based on the 1940 census data, analyzing the results.

167.   _____. "A Glimpse into the Coming Fifth Census of Brazil (Sept. 1, 1940)." Presented at the Eighth American Scientific Congress, Washington, D.C., May 10-18, 1940. Rio de Janeiro, 1940.

Includes a resumé of all censuses taken in Brazil up to 1940. Also: schedules and instructions.

168.   _____. *Recenseamento de 1940: métodos e processos.*

Materials used in taking the population census on September 1, 1940. Acquired in connection with a survey on census methods taken by the Inter-American Statistical Institute in 1944. Includes: laws and decrees, schedules and other forms, instructions, punch cards, codes, exposition and reports.

169.   Brazil. Ministério do Trabalho, Indústria e Comércio. "Recenseamento geral de 1940." *Boletim do Ministério do Trabalho, Indústria e Comércio,* v. 10, no. 118 (June 1944), pp. 267-296.

A comprehensive and fairly detailed account of the status of the census as a whole and its various segments as of the end of 1943.

170.   Felippe, José Carneiro. "O recenseamento de 1940 e o Instituto Brasileiro de Geografia e Estatística." *Revista Brasileira de Estatística,* v. 4, no. 14 (April- June 1943), pp. 193-195.

171.   Gauld, Charles A. "Brazil Takes a Census." *Journal of Geography,* v. 40, no. 4 (April 1941), pp. 138-144.

A general description of the census of 1940.

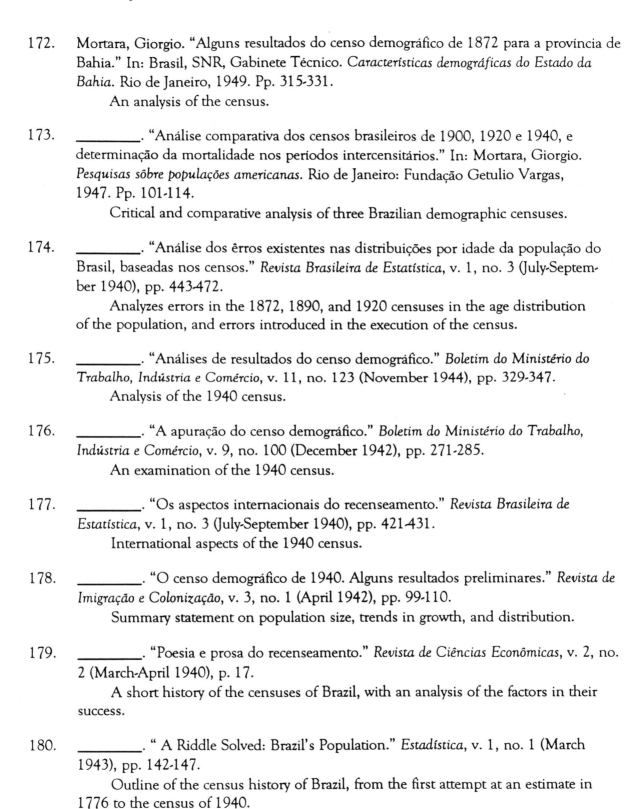

172. Mortara, Giorgio. "Alguns resultados do censo demográfico de 1872 para a província de Bahia." In: Brasil, SNR, Gabinete Técnico. *Características demográficas do Estado da Bahia.* Rio de Janeiro, 1949. Pp. 315-331.
An analysis of the census.

173. _____. "Análise comparativa dos censos brasileiros de 1900, 1920 e 1940, e determinação da mortalidade nos períodos intercensitários." In: Mortara, Giorgio. *Pesquisas sôbre populações americanas.* Rio de Janeiro: Fundação Getulio Vargas, 1947. Pp. 101-114.
Critical and comparative analysis of three Brazilian demographic censuses.

174. _____. "Análise dos êrros existentes nas distribuições por idade da população do Brasil, baseadas nos censos." *Revista Brasileira de Estatística,* v. 1, no. 3 (July-September 1940), pp. 443-472.
Analyzes errors in the 1872, 1890, and 1920 censuses in the age distribution of the population, and errors introduced in the execution of the census.

175. _____. "Análises de resultados do censo demográfico." *Boletim do Ministério do Trabalho, Indústria e Comércio,* v. 11, no. 123 (November 1944), pp. 329-347.
Analysis of the 1940 census.

176. _____. "A apuração do censo demográfico." *Boletim do Ministério do Trabalho, Indústria e Comércio,* v. 9, no. 100 (December 1942), pp. 271-285.
An examination of the 1940 census.

177. _____. "Os aspectos internacionais do recenseamento." *Revista Brasileira de Estatística,* v. 1, no. 3 (July-September 1940), pp. 421-431.
International aspects of the 1940 census.

178. _____. "O censo demográfico de 1940. Alguns resultados preliminares." *Revista de Imigração e Colonização,* v. 3, no. 1 (April 1942), pp. 99-110.
Summary statement on population size, trends in growth, and distribution.

179. _____. "Poesia e prosa do recenseamento." *Revista de Ciências Econômicas,* v. 2, no. 2 (March-April 1940), p. 17.
A short history of the censuses of Brazil, with an analysis of the factors in their success.

180. _____. " A Riddle Solved: Brazil's Population." *Estadística,* v. 1, no. 1 (March 1943), pp. 142-147.
Outline of the census history of Brazil, from the first attempt at an estimate in 1776 to the census of 1940.

181.   Pessoa, H. E. Alvim. "Compreensão e profundidade dos inquéritos censitários." *Boletim do Ministério do Trabalho, Indústria e Comércio*, v. 10, no. 116 (April 1944), pp. 280-294; v. 10, no. 117 (May 1944), pp. 263- 273.

    A retrospective summary followed by a detailed resumé of the contents of the various sections of the 1940 census.

182.   Soares, José C. de Macedo. "Estatística, geografia e o recenseamento." *Revista Brasileira de Estatística*, v. 3, no. 11 (July-September 1942), pp. 393-400.

183.   _____. "A obra de prospecção nacional do IBGE." *Revista Brasileira de Estatística*, v. 4, no. 14 (April-June 1943), pp. 179-192.

    The census of 1940 is described as one of the achievements of the Institute.

1950-1959

184.   Brazil. Instituto Brasileiro de Geografia e Estatística. *Amostragem nos censos de população e habitação*. Rio de Janeiro, 1957.

    On the use of sampling in censuses.

185.   _____. "Censo demográfico de 1950." *Revista Brasileira de Geografia*, v. 13, no. 1 (January-March 1951), pp. 127-162.

186.   _____. *Censo demográfico; instrucções ao recenseador*. Rio de Janeiro, 1959.
    Enumerator's instructions (1960 census).

187.   _____. *Censo demográfico 1960: esquema de operação*. Rio de Janeiro, 1958.
    Plan of operation for the 1960 population census.

188.   _____. *Censo experimental de Brasília; população, habitação, 17 de maio de 1959*. [Rio de Janeiro], 1959.

    Experimental census to test techniques to be employed in the national census of 1960. Introduction briefly describes operational and methodological aspects, also publication plan. Nearly three-quarters of the document consists of a lengthy, very detailed analysis of the results, including a comparison with previous censuses. A good analytical source.

189.   _____. *Documentos censitários*. Series A, B, C, and D. Rio de Janeiro, 1951. Documents used in the 1950 census. The series is organized as follows: A. Census legislation; B. Historical studies; C. Documents relating to the 1950 census; D. Studies of census methodology, etc.

190.   _____. *Elementos de amostragem probabilística aplicada aos censos.* Documentos
        Censitários, series D, no. 7. Rio de Janeiro, 1957.
        Elements of probability sampling applied to the census of 1950.

191.   _____. "As formas da declaração da idade no censo de 1950, no Distrito Federal."
        Revista Brasileira de Estatística, v. 13, no. 49 (January-March 1952), pp. 41-43.
        Patterns in the returns on age in the 1950 census, Federal District.

192.   _____. "Informação sôbre o sexto recenseamento geral do Brasil." *Revista Brasileira
        de Estatística,* v. 12, no. 48 (October-December 1951), pp. 433-446.
        Information on the 1950 census (organization, preparations, etc.).

193.   _____. *Informe sobre a execução do censo da cidade de Ituiutaba.* Rio de Janeiro, 1957.
        Describes the methods and procedures used in the census, as well as the final
        results.

194.   _____. *Investigações sôbre os recenseamentos da população geral do Império.* Rio de
        Janeiro, 1951.

195.   _____. *Notas sôbre a divulgação do recenseamento geral do 1950.* Documentos
        Censitários, series C, no. 16. [Rio de Janeiro], [n.d.].
        The publication of the 1950 census.

196.   _____. "População urbana e população rural. Problemas de definição e
        classificação. Distribuiçao da população brasileira, segundo o recenseamento de
        1940." *Revista Brasileira de Estatística,* v. 11, no. 43 (July-September 1950), pp. 432-
        465.
        Discusses urban versus rural populations, and problems of definition and clas-
        sification.

197.   _____. *Processo de amostragem proposto para o censo de população.* Rio de Janeiro,
        1958.
        Sampling procedures proposed for the 1960 population census.

198.   _____. *Programa de planejamento do recenseamento geral de 1960 . . .* Rio de Janeiro,
        1957.
        Planning program for the 1960 national census.

199.   _____. *O quesito "religião" no censo demográfico de 1950.* Rio de Janeiro, 1953.
        Questions on religion in the 1950 population census.

200.   _____. *Recenseamento geral do Brasil (1. de setembro de 1940).* Série nacional. Censo
        demográfico. Rio de Janeiro, 1950.

Describes plan of operation and publication, lists used by enumerators, questionnaires. Includes a rather detailed discussion of terms and concepts used.

201.   _____. *Resumo histórico dos inquéritos censitários realizados no Brasil*. Documentos Censitários, series B, no. 4. Rio de Janeiro, 1951.

202.   _____. *VI recenseamento geral do Brasil*. [Rio de Janeiro, 1954-1956].
Vol. 1: brief description of legal basis for census, comparison with 1940 census, lists and questionnaires used (sample attached), publication plan, discussion of basic terms and concepts used.

203.   Figueiredo, Jaime de. *Coisas que acontecem num recenseamento*. Rio de Janeiro: Instituto Brasileiro de Geografia e Estatística, 1959.
The 1940 census from a different point of view. Sample chapter headings: "The Song of the IBGE'ano," "The Census in Popular Music," "Poetry Inspired by the Census," "Sixty Census Anecdotes," "Fanaticism and Ignorance Fight Against the Census."

204.   Mortara, Giorgio. "O desenvolvimento da população prêta e parda do Brasil." In: Brasil. CNE. Laboratório de Estatística. *Estudo sôbre a natalidade e mortalidade no Brasil*. Rio de Janeiro, 1952. Pp. 35-46.
Critical and comparative analysis of the censuses of 1872, 1890, and 1940 with a view to establishing the approximate variation between various racial groups.

205.   _____. "Les erreurs dans les déclarations de l'age dans les recensements brésiliens de 1940 et 1950." Communication to the gathering of the Institut International de Statistique and the Union Internationale pour l'Etude Scientifique de la Population, Rome, September 1953. Rio de Janeiro: Instituto Brasileiro de Geografia e Estatística, 1953.

206.   _____; et al. *Observações sôbre a discriminação da população urbana no censo de 1940*. Rio de Janeiro: Instituto Brasileiro de Geografia e Estatística, 1950.
Notes on the determination of the urban population in the 1940 census.

1960-1969

207.   Borges, T. P. Accioly. "Censo demográfico de Brasília, a nova capital do Brasil." *Boletim do Centro Latino-Americano de Pesquisas en Ciências Sociais*, v. 3, no. 2 (May 1960), pp. 30-37.

208.   Brazil. Fundação Instituto Brasileiro de Geografia e Estatística. *Censo demográfico de 1960*. Rio de Janeiro, [n.d.].

Each volume has a brief introduction describing basic terms used in questionnaire; publication plan; some basic operational and methodological information. Includes sample questionnaire.

209. Hasselmann, Sergio. "Alguns aspectos do censo brasileiro de 1960." *América Latina*, v. 6, no. 2 (April-June 1963), pp. 89-106. Rio de Janeiro.

210. Marcilio, Maria-Luiza. *La ville de São Paulo: peuplement et population, 1750-1850, d'après les registres paroissiaux et les recensements anciens.* Rouen: Université de Rouen, 1968.
    Describes and evaluates some historical censuses taken in São Paulo, and analyzes their results in depth. Important historical source.

1970-1979

211. Altmann, Ana Maria Goldani; Ferreira, Carlos Eugênio de C. "Evolução do censo demográfico e registro civil como fontes de dados para a análise da fecundidade e mortalidade no Brasil." *Boletim Demográfico*, v. 10, no. 2 (October-December 1979), pp. 6-29.
    Origin and evolution of the population census in Brazil, with a special examination of the categories of fertility and mortality.

212. Balhana, Altiva Pilatti; Westphalen, Cecília Maria. "O censo dos alemães do Paraná em 1917." *Jahrbuch fur Geschichte von Staat, Wirtschaft und Gesellschaft Lateinamerikas*, v. 13 (1976), pp. 404-419.
    Discusses a 1917 census of the German population of Paraná, Brazil.

213. Barros, Ernani T. de. "Aplicações dos resultados do censo demográfico." *Revista Brasileira de Estatística*, v. 32 (April-June 1971), pp. 191-201.

214. Brazil. Fundação Instituto Brasileiro de Geografia e Estatística. "Alguns problemas nos levantamentos censitários de população." In: *Encontro brasileiro de estudos populacionais: contribuicões apresentadas.* Rio de Janeiro: Diretoria de Divulgação, 1976. Pp. 9-11.
    Statistical agency describes some problems in carrying out population censuses.

215. _____. *Censo demográfico. Brasil.* Rio de Janeiro, 1973.
    Introduction discusses briefly basic concepts and terms used in questionnaire; methodology; use of sample census; publication of results. Includes sample census schedules and other forms.

216. _____. *Contribuições para o estudo da demografia do Brasil.* Rio de Janeiro, 1970.
    Chapter 1 contains a brief evaluation of Brazilian censuses up to 1940.

217.   _____. *Metodologia do censo demográfico de 1970*. Rio de Janeiro, 1970.
        Compilation of informational material outlining the data collection methodology of the 1970 general census.

218.   Costa, Tereza Cristina N. Aráujo. "O principio classificatório 'côr', sua complexidade e implicações para um estudo censitário." *Revista Brasileira de Geografia*, v. 36, no. 3 (July-September 1974), pp. 91- 103.
        Methodology of color classifications in Brazilian censuses.

219.   Hugon, Paul. *Demografia brasileira*. São Paulo: Editora Atlas, 1973.
        Includes a brief section on the general population censuses taken in Brazil between 1872 and 1970.

220.   Irwin, Richard; Spielman, Evelyn. "Nota sôbre a subenumeração da população de menos de 10 anos de idade do Brasil." *Revista Brasileira de Estatística*, v. 34 (April-June 1973), pp. 277-280.
        Presents evidence of underenumeration based on a comparison of 1970 census data with crude birth rates for 1960-1970.

221.   Veloso, Heitor C. "O censo demográfico de 1970." *Revista Brasileira de Estatística*, v. 31 (July-September 1970), pp. 241-249.
        Briefly outlines plans for content, data collecting, processing, and publication of the 1970 census. Includes sample forms and a table comparing the 1960 and 1970 censuses in terms of questions asked.

222.   Young, Drew M. "An Evaluation of Preliminary Age and Sex Data from the 1970 Brazilian Census." *Revista Geográfica*, no. 81 (December 1974), pp. 91-104. Mexico City.
        Compares available data from the 1970 census with those of the 1960 census to determine internal consistency of the censuses.

1980-1989

223.   Associação Brasileira de Estudos Populacionais. *Censos, consensos, contra-sensos: III seminário metodológico dos censos demográficos, Ouro Prêto, junho de 1984*. São Paulo, [1984?].
        Seminar on the methodological aspects of censuses in Brazil.

224.   _____. "I seminário metodológico sôbre os censos demográficos, São Paulo, 11-13 de maio, 1983." *Informativo ABEP*, no. 19 (October-December 1983). São Paulo.
        Report from a 1983 seminar on the methodological aspects of Brazilian censuses, especially the 1980 census.

225. _____. *Sugestões ao censo demográfico de 1990*. Brasília, December 1987.
      Suggestions regarding questions to be included in the 1990 census.

226. Bercovich, Alicia M. *Utilización de los censos de población en el trabajo de cuentas nacionales*. Buenos Aires: Centro de Estudios de Población, 1986.
      Examination of an experimental program in Brazil to improve measurement of economic data in population censuses.

227. Brazil. Fundação Instituto Brasileiro de Geografia e Estatística. *Amostra de 1% dos registros do censo demográfico de 1970. Manual do usuário*. Rio de Janeiro, 1980.
      Highly technical manual of statistical procedures used in the 1970 census to calculate sample error, etc. Also includes a fairly detailed list of definitions.

228. _____. *Amostra de uso público do censo demográfico de 1980: metodologia e manual do usuário*. Rio de Janeiro, 1985.
      Description of two public use samples available from the 1980 census.

229. _____. "Comparação entre os resultados preliminares do censo demográfico de 1980 e os valores projetados da população para 1o/ix/1980." *Boletim Demográfico*, v. 11, no. 2 (October-December 1980), pp. 4-8.

230. _____. *Metodologia do censo demográfico de 1980*. Rio de Janeiro, 1983.
      In-depth discussion of the methodology of the 1980 census, including its planning, geographical basis, personnel training, data collection, quality control, statistical procedures. Includes a chapter on the history of demographic censuses in Brazil. A valuable source.

231. Costa, Luiz N. da. "Aplicação da amostragem na coleta dos censos demográficos no Brasil." *Revista Brasileira de Estatística*, v. 48, nos. 189-190 (January-December 1987), pp. 35-64.
      The data sampling methods used in recent censuses in Brazil, including the 1980 census, are reviewed and compared with the sampling methods used in the U.S., Canada, and Australia.

232. Instituto de Pesquizas Econômicas. *Investigações sôbre os recenseamentos da população geral do império e de cada provincia de per si tentados desde os tempos coloniais ate hoje. Resumo histórico dos inquéritos censitários realizados no Brasil: recenseamento do Brasil, 1920*. Sao Paulo, 1986.
      Part I consists of an analysis of available census data for Brazil in 1870. Part II reviews available census data for 1920.

233.   Lehwing, Mariene Bougeard; Vasconcellos, Mauricio Teixeira Leite de. *Cobertura no censo demográfico*. Rio de Janeiro: Fundação Instituto Brasileiro de Geografia e Estatística, 1986.
    Analysis and results of the measures taken to improve the coverage of the Brazilian 1980 census.

234.   Martine, George. "Notas sôbre os resultados preliminares do censo demográfico de 1980." Brasília, April 1981. (Mimeo.)

235.   _____; Arias, Alfonso R. "A evolução do emprego no campo." *Revista Brasileira de Estudos de População*, v. 4, no. 2 (July-December 1987), pp. 39-84.
    A comparison of data collected from population and agricultural censuses concerning agricultural employment in Brazil. The study aims to analyze the origin, form, and significance of the differences between the two censuses, in concepts, methodology, limitations, and outcome.

236.   Medici, André C. "Comparação dos conceitos e características referentes à população econômicamente ativa investigadas ao longo dos censos demográficos." *Boletim Demográfico*, v. 13, no. 1 (January-March 1982), pp. 25-41.
    An analysis of the changes in concepts and terminology used to record data on the economically active population in Brazilian censuses from 1950 to 1980.

237.   Merrick, Thomas William. *Research Opportunities and Strategies with Sample Data from the 1970 Brazilian Census*. Aguas de São Pedro [n.p.], 1980.
    Comments on the research potential of the sample (1% of the total census, made available to the public by the national census agency). Different strategies for using the sample are discussed, such as the use of subsamples, the creation of archives, and various computer applications.

238.   Rio Grande do Sul. Fundação de Economia e Estatística. *De Provincia de São Pedro a Estado do Rio Grande do Sul. Censo do Rio Grande do Sul: 1803-1950*. Pôrto Alegre, 1981.
    Mainly tables, but contains a historical section on censuses in the state, including methodology.

Chile

1850-1859

239.   Chile. Oficina Central de Estadística. *Censo jeneral de la República de Chile, levantado en abril de 1854.* Santiago: Imprenta del Ferrocarril, 1858.

Introduction contains instructions for filling out the census form, and general instructions for the administrators, including how to read the tabulated results. Briefly compares 1854 census with those of 1835 and 1843, and summarizes comments by provincial officials as to the quality of the census in their respective jurisdictions.

1860-1869

240.   Chile. Oficina Central de Estadística. *Censo jeneral de la República de Chile, levantado el 19 de abril de 1865.* Santiago: Imprenta Nacional, 1866.

Introduction contains description of census questions, explanation of tabulated results, legal basis for census, instructions on filling out forms, operational details. One chapter discusses U.S. and European censuses.

1880-1889

241.   Chile. Oficina Central de Estadística. *Sesto censo jeneral de la población de Chile, levantado el 26 de noviembre de 1885.* Valparaiso: Imprenta de la Patria, 1889.

Introduction briefly compares 1885 census with earlier ones; summarizes local officials' comments on the quality of the census in their regions; details planned procedures; instructs how to fill out forms; reproduces sample schedule.

1900-1909

242.   Chile. Oficina Central de Estadística. *Sétimo censo jeneral de la población de Chile, levantado el 28 de noviembre de 1895.* Valparaiso: Imprenta del Universo de Guillermo Helfmann, 1900.

Introduction describes how 1895 census differs from previous censuses. Also gives instructions for filling out schedules, and discusses census classifications, planned procedures, and publication plan.

243.   Magallanes Territory. *Censo jeneral de población i edificación, industria, ganadería i minería del Territorio de Magallanes, República de Chile, levantado . . . el día 8 de setiembre de 1906.* Punta Arenas: Imprenta de "El Magallanes", 1907.

Introduction describes legal basis for the census, procedures to be followed, and instructions to the enumerators, and reproduces a questionnaire and discusses the questions. One chapter analyzes the census results, with some comparison with earlier censuses.

1920-1929

244.   Chile. Dirección General de Estadística. *Censo de población de la República de Chile, levantado el 15 de diciembre de 1920.* Santiago: Universo, 1925.

Introduction discusses pre-census publicity, recruitment of personnel, and numerous other operational matters. Lists detailed instructions to enumerators. Sample schedule included.

245.   Cruchaga, Miguel. *Estudio sobre la organización económica y la hacienda pública de Chile.* Madrid: Editorial Reus, 1929.

Vol. 1, pp. 457-540, contains fairly detailed discussion of early Chilean censuses, including lists of terms and concepts, an analysis of results, and comparisons with other countries.

1930-1939

246.   Chile. Dirección General de Estadística. *Décimo censo nacional de la población, 27 de noviembre de 1930.* Folleto no. 3. "Historia y fines de los censos: los censos de Chile, sus errores; determinación de la población entre censo y censo; preparación y realización de un censo; el censo chileno de 1930." Santiago, [n.d.].

By Roberto Vergara, director of Chile's official statistical agency.

247.   _____. *Resultados del X censo de la población, efectuado el 27 de noviembre de 1930, y estadísticas comparativas con censos anteriores.* Santiago: Universo, 1931.

Introductory section describes the schedule and its questions; legal basis for census; personnel; prior advertising; compilation of results; census cost; preliminary results. Other chapters describe administrative zones for the census, and list census rules and lengthy instructions for local census administrators and enumerators regarding operational details. Includes sample questionnaire.

248.   _____. *Sinopsis geográfico-estadístico de la República de Chile.* Santiago: Universo, 1933.

Brief history of population censuses in Chile.

1940-1949

249. Chile. Dirección Nacional de Estadística. *Censo de 1940: métodos y procedimientos.*
Materials used in taking the 1940 population and housing census. Acquired in connection with a survey on census methods taken by the Inter-American Statistical Institute in 1944. Includes instructions.

250. _____. *Libreta del empadronador: XI censo de población.* Santiago: Universo, 1940.
Enumerator's booklet for the 1940 census.

251. _____. *Reglamento del XI censo de población.* Santiago, 1940.
Regulations for the execution of the population census of November 28, 1940.

252. Crocco Ferrari, Juan. *Ensayos sobre la población chilena.* Santiago: Universidad Católica, 1947.
Lists and evaluates some historical censuses. Critically examines the methodology of the 1930 and 1940 censuses, especially the classifications used for professional occupations.

253. Cuadra, Guillermo de la. "Censo de la Capitanía General de Chile." *Boletín de la Academia Chilena de la Historia,* no. 12 (1940).

254. Vergara, Roberto. "Los censos de población en Chile." Eighth American Scientific Congress, *Proceedings,* v. 8 (1942), pp. 95-108.
History, description, and evaluation (highly technical) of Chilean population censuses by the former director of the country's statistical agency.

1950-1959

255. Chile. Dirección Nacional de Estadística. *XII censo de población y I de vivienda de Chile, levantado el 24 de abril, año 1952. Métodos y procedimientos.* Santiago, 1952.
Methodology of the 1952 census.

256. Chile. Junta Gubernativa. *Censo de 1813.* Santiago: Imprenta Chile, 1953.
The introduction by Raúl Silva Castro of the Archivo Nacional discusses the 1813 census and other historical Chilean censuses.

257. Chile. Servicio Nacional de Estadística y Censos. *XII censo general de población y I de vivienda, levantado el 24 de abril de 1952.* Santiago: Empresa Periodística Gutemberg, 1956.
Vol. 1 contains a long chapter on the history of census-taking in Chile, including methodology and evaluations. A lengthy, detailed section follows, describing legal

basis of census, census cartography, administrative organization, test censuses, census schedule, training of personnel, manuals, publicity, compilation and revision of data, codification, tabulation, sample censuses, publication plan. Sample schedule is included.

258. Morales Vergara, Julio. *Análisis demográfico del censo chileno de 1920*. Santiago: Centro Latinoamericano de Demografía, 1959.

1960-1969

259. Alvarez, Leonel; Dehollain, Alejandro. *Informe sobre el censo de prueba de Rengo*. Santiago: Centro Latinoamericano de Demografía, 1960.

260. Chile. Dirección de Estadística y Censos. *Algunos resultados del XIII censo de población y II de vivienda*. Santiago, 1962.

    Introduction describes the sample and the method for obtaining it, discusses the probable maximum error (with tables), and gives the sample error equation.

261. _____. *Algunos resultados provinciales del XIII censo de población obtenidos por muestreo*. Santiago, 1963.

    Introduction discusses samples by province, sampling technique, and determination of errors in population estimates, and presents the sample error equation and other technical statistical information.

262. _____. *Breves consideraciones sobre la muestra de la población del censo de 1960, en relación a las características de edad y sexo*. Santiago, 1964.

263. _____. *XIII censo de población, 29 de noviembre de 1960. Serie A. Resumen del país*. Santiago, [196-].

    Introduction describes census organization and administration; census cartography; questionnaire; test censuses; training of personnel; publicity; data quality control; revision, codification, and verification of data; tabulation; publication plan. Half the document is a detailed analysis of the results, including a discussion of the classifications and terms used.

264. Cruz-Coke, R. "El censo de 1813 y las razas chilenas." *Revista Médica de Chile*, v. 91 (1963), pp. 931-935.

265. Gutiérrez Roldán, Héctor. "Breve análisis de las declaraciones por sexo y edad de los censos de población de Chile 1930, 1940, 1952 y 1960." In: Centro Latinoamericano de Demografía. *Chile*. Santiago, 1966.

266. Kappes Barrientos, Héctor; Marks, Eli S. "Valoración de la calidad de los censos chilenos de 1960." *Estadística*, v. 19, no. 73 (December 1961), pp. 689- 704.

      Evaluates the accuracy of the 1960 Chilean censuses. Reports on the methodology of re-enumeration tests, concentrating mainly on coverage error.

267. Mattelart, Armand. *Manual de análisis demográfico: Un ejemplo de investigación en un país latino-americano, Chile.* Santiago: Universidad Católica de Chile, 1964.

      Statistical manual for demographic analysis. Introduction surveys and critically examines censuses taken in Latin America from the turn of the century to 1960. This is followed by a general discussion of censuses, and a history of census-taking in Chile. Focusing on Chilean censuses, particularly the 1952 census, there is a lengthy chapter on the evaluation of the quality of census data. An important source, very technical, containing much information on modern Latin American censuses, especially those of Chile.

268. Morales Vergara, Julio. *Análisis demográfico del censo chileno de 1907.* Santiago: Centro Latinoamericano de Demografía, 1961. (Mimeo.)

269. Pereira Salas, Eugenio. "El desenvolvimiento histórico-étnico de la población de Chile." *Geografía Económica de Chile*, [no v.n.] (1965), pp. 337-356.

      Includes discussion of both historical and recent censuses.

1970-1979

270. Celedón, Juan Vicente. *Inconsistencias en cuatro censos chilenos a la luz del programa STAD-4.* Edmonton, Canada: University of Alberta, Department of Sociology, 1979.

      An analysis of the results obtained by applying the STAD-4 computer program (which processes census data in specific ways) to the Chilean censuses of 1940, 1952, and 1970.

271. Chile. Instituto Nacional de Estadísticas. *Censo de prueba de población y vivienda. Comuna Melipilla. 30 de noviembre de 1979.* Santiago, 1979.

      Test census prior to the 1982 national census. Four volumes include manuals and schedule.

272. _____. *Informe y análisis de resultados: 1er. censo de prueba de población y vivienda, Comuna de Buin, Chile, agosto 1978.* Santiago, 1978.

      Presentation and analysis of the results of a test census. Includes information on methodology and operational details, schedules, cartographic materials, manuals, and a critical evaluation.

273. Gutiérrez Roldán, Héctor. *La población de Chile.* Paris: Imprimerie Louis-Jean, 1975.

Chapter 1 contains a brief discussion of Chilean censuses, including estimates of error.

274.   Inter-American Statistical Institute. *Actividades estadísticas de las naciones americanas: Chile.* Washington, D.C., 1977.

275.   McCaa, Robert. "Chilean Social and Demographic History: Sources, Issues, and Methods." *Latin American Research Review*, v. 13, no. 2 (1978), pp. 104-126.
Includes discussion of historical and recent censuses, with evaluations.

1980-1989

276.   Chile. Instituto Nacional de Estadísticas. *Cédula censal.* Santiago, 1982.
Questionnaire from the 1982 census.

277.   _____. *Memoria de consultores técnicos: etapa procesamiento manual, XV censo nacional de población y IV de vivienda, mayo 1982 - abril 1983.* Santiago, 1982.
Description of the manual processing of the data from the 1982 Chilean census. Includes: personnel qualifications; codification and verification of data; organization of work groups; analysis of classification manuals; recommendations, etc.

278.   Mamalakis, Markos. *Historical Statistics of Chile, 1840-1967.* V. 2. Westport, Conn.: Greenwood Press, 1980.
Contains a section on the history, description, and critical evaluation of Chilean population censuses, and a short history of the official statistical agency. Despite its brevity, a valuable source.

279.   Tacia Chamy, Odette. *Frecuencia en la toma de información de datos censales.* Santiago: Instituto Nacional de Estadísticas, 1985.
History of population censuses in Chile.

280.   _____. *Planificación, organización, levantamiento y procesamiento del XV censo nacional de población y IV de vivienda, 1982.* Santiago: Instituto Nacional de Estadísticas, 1986.

281.   Travis, Carole. *Guide to Latin American and West Indian Census Material: A Bibliography and Union List. 2. Chile.* London: Institute of Latin American Studies, 1982.
List of known census publications, with information on their location in British libraries.

Colombia

1910-1919

282. Colombia. Ministerio de Gobierno. *Censo general de la República de Colombia, levantado el 5 de marzo de 1912.* Bogotá: Imprenta Nacional, 1912.

    Introduction describes legal basis for census, lists instructions and procedures, and specifies the information to be collected.

1930-1939

283. Colombia. Dirección General de Estadística. *Decretos y bases de organización para la ejecución de los censos.* Bogotá: Editorial "El Gráfico", 1938.

    Legislative and organizational basis for the censuses of 1938. Bound with *Instrucciones generales para la ejecución de los censos de edificios y población* (instructions to the enumerators), including an organizational chart. Census schedules bound in.

284. _____. "Informe que la Contraloría General de la República rende al Sr. Ministro de Gobierno y a las honorables Cámaras sobre el levantamiento del censo civil de 1938." *Anales de Economía y Estadística,* v. 2, no. 4 (August 1939), pp. 3-45.

    General introductory statement on organization and results of 1938 census. Part I: brief history of census-taking in Colombia and description of the preparations for the present census. Part II: legal decrees. Part III: data requested; definitions of terms. Part IV: costs; census organization. Part V: summary of data.

285. Lleras Restrepo, Carlos. *La estadística nacional: su organización, sus problemas.* Bogotá: Imprenta Nacional, 1938.

    Overview of statistics in Colombia. One chapter is devoted to population statistics and censuses: legal basis, organization, procedures. Includes discussion of the 1938 census.

286. Suárez Rivadeneira, Antonio. "Comentarios a la composición de la población colombiana, por sexo, edad y estado civil, según el censo de 1938." *Anales de Economía y Estadística,* v. 2, no. 6 (December 1939), pp. 1-15.

    An analysis of sex ratios for single years of age by marital status, followed by a detailed analysis of age pyramids and age classifications in relation to those of other countries.

1940-1949

287.   Colombia. Dirección Nacional de Estadística. *Censo general de población, 5 de julio de 1938.* . . . [By regional department.] Bogotá: Imprenta Nacional, 1940.
        Introduction lists and defines the variables investigated, describes organization and planning (including sending an official to Mexico to study Mexican census-taking), publicity, costs, compilation of results, some operational details.

288.   _____. *Censo general de población, 5 de julio de 1938.* . . . *Resumen general del país.* Bogotá: Imprenta Nacional, 1942.
        Brief general discussion of the 1938 census, followed by an analysis of the data.

289.   Higuita, Juan de Dios. "Estudio histórico analítico de la población colombiana en 170 años." *Anales de Economía y Estadística,* v. 3, no. 2 (1940). Supplement. Bogotá.
        Covers the census history of Colombia to 1940, with a critical examination of the censuses (including that of 1938).

290.   Montoya, Hernán. "El censo de 1938 fue admirablemente realizado." *Anales de Economía y Estadística,* v. 6, no. 5 (March 1943), pp. 29-37.
        Summary of the plans, execution, and general results of the 1938 census.

291.   Suárez Rivadeneira, Antonio. "Esquema del plan de organización puesto al servicio del levantamiento de los censos de edificios y población llevados a cabo en Colombia en 1938." Eighth American Scientific Congress, *Proceedings,* v. 8 (1942), pp. 93-94.
        Paper presented by the director of the Colombian national census agency.

292.   Zalamea, Jorge. "Introducción al censo de 1938." *Anales de Economía y Estadística,* v. 3, no. 3 (June 1940), pp. 75-82.

1950-1959

293.   Charry Lara, Alberto. *Desarrollo histórico de la estadística nacional en Colombia.* Bogotá: Imprenta Nacional, 1954.
        History of statistics in Colombia, published by the national statistical agency. Arranged by year. Describes each regional and national population census, with some evaluation and comments on methodology. Also specifies when and where the results were published.

294.   Colombia. Departamento Administrativo Nacional de Estadística. *Censo de población de 1951 (mayo 9).* Bogotá, 1954.
        The volumes for each regional department contain general comments, and definitions of the variables investigated.

295.   _____. "Preparación de los censos." *Boletín Mensual de Estadística*, v. 9 (September 1959), p. 3.

296.   Colombia. Dirección Nacional de Estadística. "Censo y demografía." *Boletín Mensual de Estadística*, no. 24 (February 1953), pp. 8-12, and no. 25 (March 1953), pp. 8-12.
Includes discussion of the problems of the 1951 census.

297.   Inter-American Statistical Institute. *Actividades estadísticas de las naciones americanas. Colombia.* Washington, D.C.: Pan American Union, 1956.
Describes the national statistical system, its organization and activities, and discusses the 1951 population census.

298.   Melgarejo Rey, Jesús M. "Reseña de los censos de 1951." *Economía y Estadística*, v. 4, no. 82 (1956), pp. 77-141.
Topics include: history of censuses in Colombia since 1770; organization of the 1951 census; variables investigated; the execution and tabulation of the census; publications; evaluation of quality.

299.   Ortiz C., Luis B. *La organización censal de Colombia en 1950: estudio crítico.* Bogotá: Dirección de los Censos Nacionales, 1951.

300.   Zubieta, Hernando. "Apuntes sobre la clasificación ocupacional." *Economía y Estadística*, v. 4, no. 79 (August 1954), pp. 18-34.
Occupational classifications used in the most recent population census of Colombia.

1960-1969

301.   Colombia. Departamento Administrativo Nacional de Estadística. *XIII censo nacional de población (15 de julio de 1964). Resumen general.* Bogotá: Imprenta Nacional, 1967.
Legal basis (decrees); planning, staff training, and organization; rural versus urban areas; operational details; discussion of variables and concepts; post-census sample to evaluate census accuracy; codification and tabulation; advertising; etc.

302.   Gómez, Fernando. *Análisis de los censos de población del siglo XIX en Colombia.* Bogotá: Ediciones Universidad de los Andes, 1969.
Demographic analysis of the results of Colombia's 19th century population censuses.

303.   López Toro, Alvaro. *Análisis demográfico de los censos colombianos, 1951 y 1964.* Bogotá: Ediciones Universidad de los Andes, 1968.

1970-1979

304.   Arboleda Camargo, Henrique. "Comentario sobre censos, 1898." In: Colombia. Departamento Administrativo Nacional de Estadística. *Estadísticas históricas*. Bogotá, 1975. Pp. 106-112.

   A brief discussion of population censuses in Colombia from the first one in 1770 to 1898, by the director of the national statistical agency.

305.   Asociación Colombiana para el Estudio de la Población. *La población en Colombia*. Bogotá: Impresora-Editora L. Canal, 1975.

   Includes a short history of Colombian population censuses.

306.   Bayona Nuñez, Alberto. *Cobertura del censo de población 1973*. Serie Investigaciones, no. 1. Bogotá: Pontificia Universidad Javeriana, 1977.

   Critical examination of the coverage of the 1973 census by analyzing the basic components of demographic change. Comparisons are made with 1963 data.

307.   Colombia. Departamento Administrativo Nacional de Estadística. *XIV censo nacional de población y III de vivienda, 1973. Muestra de avance. Resumen de los Departamentos*. Bogotá, 1977.

   Most valuable for its list of 73 documents used by the census agency in the 1973 census, such as guides, manuals, evaluations, etc.

308.   _____. "El censo de 1973 y el estudio del desarrollo del país." *Boletín Mensual de Estadística*, v. 26, no. 308 (March 1977), pp. 6-25.

   Deals with the methods used to estimate the amount of underenumeration in the 1973 census.

309.   _____. "La cobertura del censo de población de 1973." *Boletín Mensual de Estadística*, v. 26, no. 308 (March 1977), pp. 7-27.

   The methodology and coverage of the 1973 national census are discussed.

310.   _____. *Encuesta de evaluación del censo*. Bogotá, 1974.

   Evaluation of the 1973 census.

311.   _____. *Guía metodológica, XIV censo nacional de población y III de vivienda: cartilla 1*. Bogotá, 1973.

   The methodology of the 1973 census.

312.   _____. *Manual del recolector de áreas con población predominablemente indígena*. Bogotá, 1973.

   1973 census manual for use in predominantly Indian territory.

313.   _____. *La población en Colombia. 1973. XIV censo nacional de población y III de vivienda. Muestra de avance.* Bogotá, 1978.

Results from advance sample. Introduction discusses the sample (objectives, type, design, error, expansion, etc.), defines basic concepts, lists and discusses the variables investigated, and compares results with those of earlier censuses.

314.   _____. *Seminario sobre problemas censales: evaluación de la ejecución del proyecto.* Bogotá, [n.d.].

Evaluation of the 1973 census.

315.   Fajardo Montaña, Dario. "El censo nacional de población indígena en Colombia." *América Indígena*, v. 32, no. 4 (October-December 1972), pp. 1125-1135.

Methodological, technical, and practical difficulties of the national census of the Indian population.

316.   Gómez, Fernando. "Los censos en Colombia antes de 1905." In: Urrutia, Miguel; Arrubla, Mario. *Compendio de estadísticas históricas de Colombia.* Bogotá: Talleres Salesianos San José, 1970. Pp. 9-31.

Describes and evaluates early population censuses in Colombia.

317.   González R., L. E. *XIV censo de población y III de vivienda, octubre 24, 1973: cobertura censal.* Bogotá: Departamento Administrativo Nacional de Estadística, 1976.

A summary of the most important methodological aspects of the census, and of the results.

318.   Hernández García, Alberto; Florez Nieto, Carmen Elisa; Cordi de Cuevas, Angela. *Análisis demográfico del Departamento del Meta, período 1964-1973.* Bogotá: Ediciones Universidad de los Andes, 1978.

One chapter contains a general analysis and extensive evaluation of each of the two censuses, with estimates of error. Also a comparative analysis of the results.

319.   Mendez Heilman, Regina; Banguero Lozano, Harold. *La calidad del censo de población de Colombia, 1973: errores de clasificación y comparación con los censos 1938-1964.* Bogotá: Ediciones Universidad de los Andes, 1979.

320.   Olivares, Juan. *Proyecciones de la población del distrito especial de Bogotá, 1965-1985.* Bogotá: Ediciones Universidad de los Andes, 1970.

Includes a brief discussion of the 1951 and 1964 census data, focusing on Bogotá.

321.   Potter, Joseph; Ordoñez, Myriam. "The Completeness of Enumeration in the 1973 Census of the Population of Colombia." *Population Index*, v. 42, no. 3 (July 1976), pp. 377-403.

    Authors discuss fertility and mortality in Colombia, based on registration data. After correcting the 1964 census data they estimate the completeness of the enumeration in the 1973 census.

322.   Quick, Sylvia. *Colombia*. Washington, D.C.: U.S. Bureau of the Census, 1979.

    Demographic information on Colombia for the period 1964-1979. Includes a critical examination of census data, with special reference to the high degree of under-enumeration.

1980-1989

323.   Colombia. Departamento Administrativo Nacional de Estadística. "Ajuste por cobertura de la población del XIV censo nacional de población y III de vivienda, el 24 de octubre de 1973." *Boletín Mensual de Estadística*, no. 355 (February 1981), pp. 4-116.

    The methodology used to adjust data from the 1973 census is described, and then used to prepare revised census totals for the country. Estimates of the completeness of the census coverage are also presented.

324.   _____. *Así será el censo 85*. Bogotá, 1985.

    General comments on the 1985 census: its utility, the organization and technology needed, the publication of results.

325.   _____. *XV censo nacional de población y IV de vivienda. V. II: Metodología*. Bogotá, 1986.

    Detailed description of the methodology of the 1985 census, including four prior test censuses and one post-census survey conducted to evaluate census coverage.

326.   _____. *Proyecto de automatización de cartografía censal*. Bogotá, 1985. (Mimeo.)
    Description of the process of computerizing the census cartography.

327.   Ferro Calvo, Mauricio. *Digitalización cartográfica: documento metodológico*. Bogotá: Departamento Administrativo Nacional de Estadística, 1985.

    Methodological description of the process of cartographic digitalization to be used in the Colombian census of 1985.

328.   Florez Nieto, Carmen Elisa; Echeverri Perrico, Rafael. *Seminario taller sobre el XV censo nacional de población y IV de vivienda, 1985*. Bogotá: Departamento Administrativo Nacional de Estadística, 1986.

Census results and their implications are examined, focusing on methodology and how to improve future censuses.

329.   García Castro, Arturo G. *Integración y capacitación del personal en el X censo general de población y vivienda 1980: Colombia*. México, D.F.: Coordinación General del Sistema Nacional de Información, 1986.
Detailed description of the different levels of census personnel, the qualifications and experience required, and the training for each level.

Ecuador

1930-1939

330.   Ecuador. Dirección General de Estadística. "Organización, iniciativas y proceso de trabajos estadísticos y censales en 1938." *Estadística y Censos*, v. 1, no. 1 (March 1939), pp. 3-35.
Organization, initiation, and progress of the statistical work on the planned census of 1938.

331.   Paz y Miño, Luis T. *La población del Ecuador*. Quito: Talleres Gráficos Nacionales, 1936.
A discussion of 18th and especially 19th century population censuses in Ecuador, with some evaluation and analysis.

1950-1959

332.   Bermeo C., Jack. "Censos del Ecuador para 1960." *Boletín Trimestral de Información Económica*, v. 10, no. 34 (January-December 1957), pp. 5-23.

333.   Ecuador. Núcleo de Estadísticos del Ecuador. Comisión de Censos. *Los censos de población, habitación y agropecuario de 1960*. Quito, 1957.
Discusses censuses that are going to be taken; dates; program and scheduling of work; organization; budgets; personnel.

334.   Santiana, Antonio. "El censo demográfico del Ecuador." *Filosofía, Letras y Ciencias de la Educación*, v. 3, no. 8 (October 1950), pp. 75-88.
Considers the position of the Indians.

1960-1969

335.   Ecuador. Dirección General de Estadística y Censos. *Primer censo de población del Ecuador, 1950. Resumen de características.* Quito, 1960.
        Introduction briefly discusses basic census classifications and concepts. Previous volumes, which contain the tabulated results for each census category, also briefly analyze these results.

336.   Ecuador. Junta Nacional de Planificación y Coordinación. División de Estadística y Censos. *Segundo censo de población y primer censo de vivienda, 25 de noviembre de 1962. Provincias.* Quito, 1964- .
        Introductory discussion of basic concepts and definitions.

337.   Inter-American Statistical Institute. *Actividades estadísticas de las naciones americanas. Ecuador.* Washington, D.C.: Pan American Union, 1963.
        Contains a section on censuses, including fairly detailed descriptions of local and national censuses and their resulting publications, with some discussion of methodology.

338.   Merlo Jaramillo, Pedro. *Evaluación y ajuste de los censos de población de 1950 y 1962.* Santiago: Centro Latinoamericano de Demografía, 1962.

339.   Nieto T., Bolívar. *Algunos aspectos relacionados con la planificación del segundo censo nacional de población del Ecuador.* Santiago: Centro Latinoamericano de Demografía, 1960. (Mimeo.)

340.   Saunders, J. V. D. *The People of Ecuador: A Demographic Analysis.* Gainesville: University of Florida Press, 1961.
        Evaluation and analysis of the 1950 national census.

341.   United Nations. Economic Commission for Latin America. *Case Studies of Arrangements for Evaluation and Utilization of Population Census Results. Report III—The Republic of Ecuador.* New York: United Nations ST/SOA/Ser. R/3, 1960.

1970-1979

342.   Ecuador. Instituto Nacional de Estadística y Censos. *El censo de población, 1974. Resultados definitivos. Resumen nacional.* Quito, 1977.
        Introduction defines basic concepts and variables investigated. Sample schedule included.

343.   _____. *Censos de población y vivienda, Ecuador 1974. Sistema audiovisual para entrenamiento de empadronadores.* Quito, 1979.

      Five separate documents describe the audiovisual system for the training of census enumerators, and evaluate its application and usefulness.

344.   Ecuador. Oficina de los Censos Nacionales. *Carchi. Quito: Junta Nacional de Planificación,* 1975.

      Describes how the personnel of the 1973 census verified every geographical name and feature in the province of Carchi to produce very accurate census maps.

345.   Hamerley, Michael T. "Quantifying the Nineteenth Century: The Ministry Reports and Gazettes of Ecuador as Quantitative Sources." *Latin American Research Review,* v. 13, no. 2 (1978), pp. 138-156.

      Section on demography evaluates 19th century population censuses.

1980-1989

346.   Ecuador. Instituto Nacional de Estadística y Censos. *IV censo de población 1982. Resultados definitivos. Resumen nacional.* Quito, 1985.

      Introduction defines basic concepts used, and includes sample schedule.

347.   _____. *Evaluación de los censos nacionales de población y vivienda de 1974.* Quito, 1980.

348.   Ortiz Mejía, Corina del Pilar. *Ecuador: preferencia de dígitos en la declaración de la edad en los censos 1974 y 1982: trabajo final de investigación.* Santiago: Centro Latinoamericano de Demografía, 1985.

      A critical examination of the last two censuses in Ecuador indicates that there are still serious errors in the declaration of age, especially among women.

Guyana

1970-1979

349.   Jamaica. University of the West Indies. Census Research Programme. *1970 Population Census of the Commonwealth Caribbean, 7 April and 25 October.* Kingston: The Herald Limited, 1973.

Vol. 1 describes the methodology employed at all stages, district boundaries, staff training, coding and checking procedures, etc.

Paraguay

1930-1939

350. Paraguay. Dirección Nacional de Estadística. *Censo de 1936: métodos y procedimientos.*
      Materials used in taking the 1936 census. Acquired in connection with a survey on census methods taken by the Inter-American Statistical Institute in 1944. Consist of: correspondence, laws and decrees, schedules, instructions, forms, reports.

1950-1959

351. "Amplitud y contenido del próximo censo nacional de población y vivienda." *Revista del Centro de Estudiantes de Ciencias Económicas,* v. 12, no. 103 (1950). Asunción.

1960-1969

352. Mellon, Roger; Silvero, Arnaldo. *Evolución de los censos de población levantados en la República del Paraguay 1950-1962.* Asunción: Secretaría Técnica de Planificación, 1965.

353. Ortiz, José C. "En torno al censo de 1946." *Revista Alcor,* no. 21 (1962), p. 3. Asunción.

1970-1979

354. Kegler de Galeano, Anneliese. "Alcance histórico-demográfico del censo de 1846. " *Revista Paraguaya de Sociología,* v. 13, no. 35 (January-April 1976), pp. 71- 121.
      Examines the 1846 census, its methodology and findings.

355. Palau Viladesau, Tomás; Galeano, Luis A. *Análisis conceptual de las categorías censales y comparabilidad entre los censos de 1950, 1962 y 1972 en Paraguay.* Asunción: Centro Paraguayo de Estudios Sociológicos, 1979.
      In addition to analyzing and comparing the three censuses, the authors also put forward recommendations to improve the quality of the 1980 census.

356. Paraguay. Dirección General de Estadística y Censos. *Censo nacional de población y viviendas, 1972.* Asunción, 1975-1976.

357. Rivarola, Domingo M.; Corvalán, Graziella; Fogel, Ramón; et al. *La población del Paraguay.* Asunción: Centro Paraguayo de Estudios Sociológicos, 1974.

    A description of some censuses, followed by an interpretation of recent census data from various demographic perspectives. Finally, a complete listing of all national and local censuses taken in Paraguay.

358. Williams, John H. "Observations on the Paraguayan Census of 1846." *Hispanic-American Historical Review,* v. 56, no. 3 (1976), pp. 424-437.

    Reviews methodology and results of the 1846 population census. Examines methods used for providing information lacking in census figures.

1980-1989

359. Paraguay. Dirección General de Estadística y Censos. *Censo nacional de población y viviendas, 1982.* Asunción, 1985.

    Contains basic definitions and concepts, brief description of procedures used, and a limited commentary on the most significant demographic changes that have taken place in the last decade. Mentions a test census. Includes sample questionnaire and graphs.

360. _____. *Censo nacional de población y viviendas 1982. Manual del empadronador.* Asunción, 1982.

    Enumerator's manual used in the 1982 census.

361. Paraguay. Instituto Paraguayo del Indígena. *Censo y estudio de la población indígena del Paraguay, 1981.* Asunción, 1982.

    Results and analysis of the first census of Paraguay's Indian population. Operational details are described, such as the design of the questionnaire, the organization of the field work, and codification of data.

Peru

1860-1869

362. Fuentes, Manuel A. *Estadística general de Lima.* Paris: Ad. Lainé et J. Havard, 1866.

    Vol. 1 contains a brief discussion of a 19th century population census of Lima.

1870-1879

363.   Paz Soldán, Mariano Felipe. *Diccionario geográfico estadístico del Perú, contiene además la etimología aymara y quechua de las principales poblaciones, lagos, ríos, cerros, etc.* Lima: Imprenta del Estado, 1877.

Contains a section on the census history of Peru.

1900-1909

364.   Peru. [Ministerio de Fomento.] *Censo de la provincia constitucional del Callao, 20 de junio de 1905.* Lima: Imprenta y Librería de San Pedro, 1906.

History of previous censuses in the province; maps and operational reports from each zone; list of personnel; instructions to and training of enumerators and inspectors; advance publicity; instructions to the public for filling out questionnaires; sample forms and schedules. Partly in French.

1920-1929

365.   Peru. Ministerio de Fomento. *Resúmenes del censo de las provincias de Lima y Callao, levantado el 17 de diciembre de 1920.* Lima: Imprenta Torres Aguirre, 1921.

Introductory section contains legal decrees, and a discussion of the preparatory work, census personnel, a test census, census schedules, margin of error, the execution of the census, some problems encountered.

1930-1939

366.   Arana Sialer, Andrés. "El censo de población y ocupación." *Gaceta Económica y Financiera,* v. 1, no. 1 (1939), pp. 4-14.

The 1940 demographic census.

367.   Herrera, Gonzalo. "El censo y la estadística." Sociedad Geográfica de Lima, *Boletín,* v. 4 (1938).

368.   Reátegui, H. Ladislao. "Importancia del censo: su funcionamiento en Loreto." *Gaceta Económica y Financiera,* no. 2 (1939), p. 4.

1940-1949

369.   Arca Parró, Alberto. "Censo nacional de población y ocupación de 1940." *Revista de Hacienda,* v. 6 (1941), pp. 121-186.

370.   _____. "Census of Peru, 1940." *Geographical Review*, v. 32, no. 1 (January 1942), pp. 1-20.

The technical advisor to the official census committee describes the plan of organization, execution, general results, and publication of the census of 1940.

371.   _____. "La ciudad capital de la República y el censo nacional de 1940." *Estadística Peruana*, v. 1, no. 1 (January 1945), pp. 24-29.

Brief discussion and analysis of the census with respect to Lima.

372.   _____. "El plan censal peruano. Etapas de su desarrollo; proyecciones de su ejecución." *Revista de Hacienda*, v. 2 (1940), pp. 115-137.

Description of the legal and administrative basis, and the actual execution of the 1940 census. Preliminary results for Lima, with comparable data from earlier censuses.

373.   _____. "Problemas y soluciones para el censo demográfico peruano de 1940." Eighth American Scientific Congress, *Proceedings*, v. 8 (1942), pp. 17-27.

The history of Peruvian population censuses, followed by a description of the methodology of the 1940 census, with recommendations for improvements for future censuses.

374.   _____. "Sinopsis histórica de los censos en el Perú." *Historia*, no. 6 (January-June 1944). Lima.

Historical resumé of the censuses of Peru.

375.   García Frias, R. "Sinopsis del crecimiento de la población del Perú y determinación del coeficiente de omisión censal." *Informaciones sociales*, v. 5, no. 7 (July 1941).

Summary of the increase in population, and determination of the coefficient of omission in the census.

376.   Lassus Arevalo, Carlos E. "Aumenta de la 'fuerza demográfica' de Lima, comparando la 'pirámide de vida' de 1931 con la de 1876." *Boletín de la Comisión Central del Censo* (April 1940), pp. 1-4.

377.   _____. "Las enfermedades profesionales y el censo de 1940." *Revista Mensual del Comercio del Perú*, no. 210 (February 1940), p. 6.

378.   Luna Vegas, Ricardo. "La estadística peruana en el sexenio 1938-1944." *Estadística*, v. 2, no. 8 (December 1944), pp. 498-505.

A history of Peruvian statistics. Includes a brief discussion of the census law of 1938, the census organization, and the planning and execution of the 1938 census.

379.   _____. "La investigación sobre las ocupaciones en el censo nacional de población. Formulación y finalidad de las preguntas en las cédulas de empadronamiento." *Boletín de la Comisión Central del Censo* (March 1940), pp. 1-3.

380.   Peru. Dirección Nacional de Estadística. *Censo general de 1940: resultados generales. Primer informe oficial.* Lima, 1941.

        Contents: Census decrees and plans, organization and execution of the census, plans for analysis and publication, estimates of omissions, analysis of results.

381.   _____. *Censo nacional de población y ocupación, 1940. Primer volumen. Resúmenes generales.* Lima: Imprenta Torres Aguirre, 1944.

        The first 200 pages, "Exposición y comentarios," present a descriptive and analytical treatment of the 1940 census. Chapter I. General discussion of the census; II. Detailed history of census-taking in Peru, with a bibliography; III. Organizational basis of the census; IV. Preparatory work (planning, cartography, etc.); V. Discussion of schedules and basic concepts; VI. Execution of census; VII. Post-census tabulation; VIII. General results; IX. Discussion of statistical procedures (the coefficient of omission); X. Detailed comparison with previous Peruvian and foreign censuses, and lengthy analysis of the results. Sixty Appendices contain documents pertaining to the census, e.g. rules, laws, cost of the census, sample schedules, instructions, official communications, etc. Appendix 58 is an annotated bibliography of the 17 most important pamphlets and booklets on the census published by the census commission. A very valuable source.

382.   _____. *Extracto estadístico del Perú, 1939.* Lima: Imprenta Americana, 1940.

        The introductory statement on population discusses the 1940 census.

383.   Stessin, Laurence. "El más grande censo de la historia." *Estadística Peruana*, no. 6 (March 1948), pp. 97-100.

384.   Uriarte, Carlos A. "Antecedentes históricos sobre la demografía nacional." *Estadística Peruana*, v. 2, no. 4 (July 1946), pp. 67-84.

        History of population statistics (including censuses) in Peru.

385.   _____. "Un ensayo de la distribución de los habitantes de Lima, ciudad capital, por grupos socio-económicos. Algo sobre el método de la 'muestra'." *Estadística Peruana*, v. 4, no. 6 (March 1948), pp. 40-56.

386.   Zavala, Graciela. "El censo municipal del Distrito de San Isidro." *Estadística Peruana*, v. 4, no. 6 (March 1948), pp. 91-96.

Report on a municipal census taken to examine changes having occurred since the 1940 census, by a official from that census. A sample of the population of Lima. Brief discussion of procedures; census form included.

1950-1959

387. Rey Riveros, Edmundo. "El censo y los aborígenes selvícolas de nuestra Amazonia." *Revista Militar del Perú*, nos. 632-634 (July-October 1956).

The census and the forest-dwelling Indians of Amazonia.

1960-1969

388. Peru. Dirección Nacional de Estadística y Censos. *VI censo nacional de población, [1 de julio de 1961]*. Lima, 1965-[1966].

Vol. 5, according to the publication plan, was projected to analyze the results of the 1961 census, and vol. 6 was to describe the census guidelines and methodology.

1970-1979

389. Centro de Estudios de Población y Desarrollo. *Informe demográfico: Perú 1970*. Lima: Tipografía Lesator, 1972.

Extensive demographic analysis based on the censuses of 1876, 1940, and 1961. One chapter examines in detail the questionnaires of each of these censuses to check comparability of data. Also contains general information pertaining to each census.

390. Peru. Dirección General de Censos, Encuestas y Demografía. *VIII censo de población y III de vivienda*. Lima, 1979.

Program, definitions and concepts, and schedules to be used in the 1981 census.

391. Peru. Instituto Nacional de Estadística. *Censo experimental de población y vivienda, Distrito de Imperial–1978*. Lima, 1978.

A complete description in 15 volumes of the planning, organization, methodology, execution, supervision, and evaluation of an experimental census taken in a district of Lima in 1978. Includes sample schedule and manuals.

392. Peru. Oficina Nacional de Estadística. *Censos nacionales: VIII de población y III de vivienda*. Lima, 1979.

A four-volume collection of materials to be used in the 1981 census.

393. _____. *Censos nacionales: VIII de población y III de vivienda: censo experimental, provincia de Cajabamba.* Lima, 1979.

  Schedules and manuals are published in six separate documents.

394. Peru. Oficina Nacional de Estadística y Censos. *Censos nacionales, VII de población, II de vivienda, 4 de junio de 1972. Resultados definitivos, nivel nacional.* Lima: Imprenta del Colegio Militar Leoncio Prado, 1974.

  Introduction briefly discusses basic definitions and concepts and lists methodological and operational highlights (organization, publicity, test census, recruitment of personnel, etc.).

395. _____. *La población del Perú.* Lima, 1974.

  Appendix 1 lists and describes Peruvian population censuses from the first one in 1876.

1980-1989

396. Duenas Cabrera, Julio. *Evaluación y corrección de la declaración de la edad en el censo de población de Perú 1981: trabajo de investigación.* Santiago: Centro Latinoamericano de Demografía, 1985. (Mimeo.)

  The error in declaration of age in the 1981 census is calculated, and found to be smaller than in the previous census.

397. Fernández Baca de Valdez, Graciela. *Perú: uso del muestreo en los censos nacionales de población y vivienda de 1981.* Lima: Instituto Nacional de Estadística, 1986.

  Describes the use of sampling in the 1981 Peruvian census, including its objectives and methodology. The results are compared with those of the total census and with an earlier test census.

398. Peru. Consejo Nacional de Población. *Perú: hechos y cifras demográficas.* Lima, 1984.

  Contains a list of population censuses from the first in 1876, with a brief description of each.

399. Peru. Instituto Nacional de Estadística. *Censos nacionales: VIII de población y III de vivienda.* Lima, 1981.

  In 14 volumes, the schedules and operational manuals used in carrying out the 1981 census.

400. _____. *Censos nacionales, VIII de población, III de vivienda, 12 de julio de 1981. Resultados definitivos de las variables investigadas por muestreo. V. 1. Nivel nacional.* Lima: Oficina de Comunicación, Información e Impresiones, 1984.

Introduction lists earlier censuses, discusses the sample (selection, sample units, relative error, etc.), lists and defines the variables investigated in the census, and discusses operational matters.

401.   _____. *Censos nacionales, VIII de población, III de vivienda, 12 de julio de 1981. Resultados definitivos, nivel nacional.* Lima, 1984.

Introduction presents the history of census-taking in Peru; a comparative analysis of results from previous censuses; definitions of the variables investigated (basic concepts); a brief commentary on methodology, planning, and operational details.

Surinam

Since independence in 1975 there has been only one census, in 1980. No sources were located.

Uruguay

1900-1909

402.   "Censos de población de la República (1852, 1860 y 1900)." *Anuario Estadístico de la República Oriental del Uruguay*, v. 1 (1905), pp. 39-116.

The results of three national censuses published with introductory remarks and some explanatory footnotes.

1910-1919

403.   "Censo general de la República en 1908." *Anuario Estadístico de la República Oriental del Uruguay*, v. 2, part 3 (1911).

Introduction discusses censuses in other countries, analyzes the 1908 results, and compares them with foreign censuses.

1950-1959

404.   Fernández, Alfredo. "Censo nacional de población." *Revista de Economía*, [no v.n.] (June-August 1954). Montevideo.

       Traces the development of the national statistical system of Uruguay from the last general population census in 1908 to 1954, and mentions repeated efforts to get a census program underway.

405.   Meyer, Morton A.; Jiménez Castro, Wilburg. *Proyecto de tabulación del censo de población de la República Oriental del Uruguay y del Departamento de Montevideo*. Montevideo, 1955.

       Proposed tabular forms for the 1956 census by department.

406.   Miller, Juan E. *Política de censos, apuntes*. Montevideo: Impresora Uruguaya, 1952.

       Notes on census policy in Uruguay.

1960-1969

407.   Rojas Molina, Omar. "El censo de población en la República Oriental del Uruguay." *Estadística*, v. 22 (June 1964), pp. 272-293.

       Notes on the background of census-taking in Uruguay. Description of legal basis, preliminary work, organization of enumeration, processing of data, and publication plans for the 1963 census. Summary of results.

408.   Uruguay. Dirección Nacional de Estadística y Censos. *Un ensayo de evaluación del IV censo general de población (encuesta de cobertura)*. Montevideo, 1965.

       Evaluation of the fourth population census, especially with regard to its coverage.

409.   _____. *Muestra de anticipación de resultados censales. IV censo general de población y II de vivienda. 16 de octubre de 1963*. [Montevideo, 1964 or 5.]

       Advance sample of census results. Introduction discusses this statistical procedure (its advantages, optimum size, calculation of absolute and relative error, controls). The census is compared with previous censuses, and efforts to ensure its quality and integrity are described. The results are analyzed and compared with those of other countries, category by category.

410.   Uruguay. Junta Asesora de Estadística y Censos. *Primer Congreso Nacional de Estadística (13 al 17 de diciembre de 1965). Recomendaciones*. [n.p., n.d.] [Source: *Population Index*, v. 33, no. 3, p. 453.]

       The first recommendation concerns statistical methods for census operations.

1970-1979

411. Centro Latinoamericano de Demografía. *Primeros resultados del análisis de la información censal del Uruguay*. Santiago, 1977.
Preliminary analysis of a sample taken in connection with the May 1975 population census. Includes a comparison with the 1963 census data.

412. Petrucelli, José L. "Uruguay, situación demográfica." In: *Uruguay, datos básicos*. Montevideo: Fundación de Cultura Universitaria, 1976. Pp. 3-34.
Briefly compares the preliminary results of 1975 census with those of 1963.

413. Universidad de la República de Uruguay. Instituto de Estadística. *Estimación de la población intercensal 1963-1975*. Montevideo, 1977.
Describes the methodology used to estimate omissions and under-registration in the two censuses.

414. Uruguay. Dirección Nacional de Estadística y Censos. *Encuesta de cobertura; 5o censo general de población y 3o de vivienda*. Montevideo [n.d.].
Evaluation of the 1975 population census based on a coverage survey carried out parallel with the census for quality control purposes.

415. _____. *Plan preliminar de tabulaciones del V censo general de población y III de viviendas, año 1975*. [n.p., n.d.] [Source: *Population Index*, v. 43, no. 1, p. 141.]
Directions for tabulating the census by age, sex, and marital status.

1980-1989

416. Klaczko, Jaime. *El Uruguay de 1908: su contexto urbano-rural, antecedentes y perspectivas*. Montevideo: Centro de Informaciones y Estudios del Uruguay, 1981.
One chapter describes Uruguayan censuses from 1852 to the present.

417. Rial Roade, Juan. *Estadísticas históricas del Uruguay, 1850-1930: población, producción agropecuaria, comercio, industria, urbanización, comunicaciones, calidad de vida*. Montevideo: Centro de Informaciones y Estudios del Uruguay, 1980.

418. _____. "Sources for Studies of Historical Demography in Uruguay (1728-1860)." *Latin American Research Review*, v. 15, no. 2 (1980), pp. 180-200.
Touches on 20th century censuses.

419. Uruguay. Dirección General de Estadística y Censos. *Boleta censal*. Montevideo, 1985.
The questionnaire used in the 1985 general census.

420.   _____. *Censo experimental de Pan de Azúcar (Depto de Maldonado) Oct. 1984*. Montevideo, 1984.

In two volumes, a general discussion of a 1984 Uruguayan test census, and a codification manual.

421.   _____. *Censos de población: análisis de su validez como instrumento para la medición de algunas características económicas*. Buenos Aires: Centro de Estudios de Población, 1986.

The validity of the census for measuring economic characteristics is tested by comparing census results with previous surveys carried out in Uruguay.

422.   _____. *Informe sobre el censo de población del Uruguay a realizarse en 1985*. Montevideo, 1985. (Mimeo.)

Proposed plan for the 1985 census.

423.   _____. *Muestra de anticipación de resultados censales. Censo general, VI de población, IV de viviendas, octubre 1985*. Montevideo, 1987.

In advance of complete results, the results of a sample are presented. Vol. 1 describes the methodology of the sample (its design, estimates of error, variation, and other technical details). Vol. 2 lists basic definitions, and analyzes the results.

Venezuela

1870-1879

424.   *Primeras actas del Ejecutivo Federal para la estadística de Venezuela*. Caracas: Imprenta Nacional, por Jesus María Monasterios, 1871. (Reprinted by Ediciones Centenario de la Dirección General de Estadística y Censos Nacionales, Caracas, 1973.)

The official plan to create a national statistical agency. One article provides for taking a population census, specifying what information is to be sought.

425.   Venezuela. Dirección General de Estadística. *Memoria de la Dirección General de Estadística al Presidente de los Estados Unidos de Venezuela en 1873*. Maracaibo: Picón, 1873.

Summary of the many population estimates and censuses of the late colonial and early national period. Includes discussion of validity and methodology.

1940-1949

426. Alvarado Franquiz, Juan. *Comentarios al VII censo de población de Venezuela, 1941.* Dirección General de Estadística. Caracas: Editorial Grafolit, 1947.

Analyzes the results of the 1941 census. (This essay also appears in the last volume of the official census publication.)

427. Boggio, Juan M. "Breves comentarios sobre los resultados preliminares del séptimo censo nacional de población." *Revista de Fomento*, v. 4 (April-June 1942), pp. 77-81.

428. Venezuela. Dirección General de Estadística. *Censo de 1941: métodos y procedimientos.*

Materials used in the population census of December 7, 1941. Acquired in connection with a survey on census methods taken by the Inter-American Statistical Institute in 1944. Contents: correspondence, instructions, expositions and reports, punch cards, codes and schedules, other forms.

429. _____. *Séptimo censo general de población, levantado el 7 de diciembre de 1941. Resumen general de la República.* Caracas: Editorial Grafolit, 1947.

Describes organization of census; basic terms and concepts used; personnel training; distribution of census materials; advertising; compilation of data and other operational details; publication of results; analysis of results.

430. _____. *Séptimo censo nacional de población 1941, instrucciones y modelos.* Caracas: Casa de Especialidades, 1941.

431. _____. *Sexto censo de población, 1936.* Caracas: Tipografía Garrido, 1940.

Brief analysis of results, including comparisons with previous Venezuelan and foreign censuses.

1950-1959

432. Venezuela. Dirección General de Estadística y Censos Nacionales. *Censo nacional de 1950. Empadronamiento especial de la población indígena.* Caracas, [1959?].

Introduction discusses previous Indian censuses, operational details of the present census, basic definitions, and the results. Appendix contains several sample questionnaires and administrative census forms, and instructions for filling them out.

433. _____. *Octavo censo general de población, 26 de noviembre de 1950. Resumen general de la República.* Caracas: Gráfica Americana, 1957.

Introduction describes legal basis, census agencies, census plan, advertising, confidentiality of data, information requested in questionnaire, list of basic terms and concepts used.

1960-1969

434. Inter-American Statistical Institute. *Actividades estadísticas de las naciones americanas. Venezuela.* Washington, D.C.: Pan American Union, 1966.
Focuses on statistics generally, but also has a section on censuses. The census history of Venezuela is presented, and there is a discussion of the 1961 census (personnel, data requested, sample survey), legal basis for census-taking, and the structure of the national statistical agency.

435. Ochoa, Elena de; Vildosolo, Reyes; Pizzi, Mario. "Análisis crítico de los datos de población existente en Venezuela: censos y Registro Civil." Paper presented at the III Congreso Venezolano de Salud Pública, Caracas, March 1966. (Mimeo.)

436. Páez Celis, Julio. *Determinación de la omisión del censo de 1961 y de las defunciones del período 1950-1961.* Caracas: Dirección General de Estadística y Censos Nacionales, 1963.
Calculates the omissions in the 1961 census, and deaths in the period 1950-1961.

437. _____. "Evaluación de las omisiones de los censos de los años 1936, 1941 y 1950 y de la omisión de las declinaciones en los feriados 1936-1941 y 1941-1950." *Revista de Fomento*, no. 97 (1962).

438. Venezuela. Dirección General de Estadística y Censos Nacionales. *Noveno censo general de población (26 de febrero de 1961). Resumen general de la República.* Caracas: Taller Gráfico de la Oficina Central del Censo, 1967.

439. _____. *Programa censal de 1960. Empadronamiento especial de la población indígena.* Caracas, 1963.

1970-1979

440. Carruyo, D.; Arrias, A. *Estado Zulia, evaluación y ajuste del censo de 1971.* Maracaibo: Universidad del Zulia, Facultad de Ciencias Económicas y Sociales, 1972. (Mimeo.)

441. Chen, Chi-Yi; Picouet, Michel. *Dinámica de la población. Caso de Venezuela.* Caracas: Universidad Católica Andrés Bello, 1979.

In-depth analysis of the population of Venezuela, based on the most recent censuses. Contains many detailed, highly technical studies of the censuses (statistical procedures used, evaluation, etc.). A major work, the most comprehensive and extensive demographic study of Venezuela available.

442. Rodríguez, Manuel Alfredo. *La estadística en la historia de Venezuela*. Caracas: Ediciones Centenario de la Dirección General de Estadísticas y Censos Nacionales, 1974.

The history of statistics in Venezuela, with an emphasis on population censuses.

443. Ruiz Guzmán, Sonia. "Notas sobre los censos venezolanos." *Estadística Venezolana*, no. 9 (January 1977), pp. 121-124.

Brief description of the principal characteristics and variables investigated in Venezuelan censuses between 1873 and 1971.

444. Venegas Borges, Pedro Luis. *El sistema estadística nacional: una institución en crisis*. [Caracas: Dirección General de Estadística y Censos Nacionales], 1974.

The director of Venezuela's official statistical agency examines the country's various statistical programs. One chapter deals with the census program, from an organizational/administrative point of view.

445. Venezuela. Dirección General de Estadística y Censos Nacionales. *Décimo censo de población y vivienda, 1971. Resumen general*. Caracas, 1976- .

446. Venezuela. Oficina Central de Estadística e Informática. *Primer censo experimental de población y vivienda. Municipio La Victoria, Estado Apagua*. Caracas, 1978.

The last 15 volumes of the Venezuelan census agency's 20-volume plan for the 1980 general census (item 447) consist of a description of a planned experimental census. The purpose was to test procedures and models to be used in the national census. The test census was planned in two stages: first a complete enumeration requesting certain basic data, and then a sample census to verify the coverage of the first one.

447. _____. *Programa censal de 1980*. Caracas, 1979.

A description in 20 volumes of the planned 1980 census. The first five volumes give information on census organization, methodology, cartographic plans, classifications, etc. Prior to the national census two test censuses were to be taken (see item 446). A subsequent sample census was planned to evaluate the quality of the national census and to obtain more detailed data on certain selected subjects.

1980-1989

448.   Bidegain Greising, Gabriel; Suárez, María Matilde. *Estimación de la tasa de omisión en el XI censo de población y vivienda.* Caracas: Universidad Católica Andrés Bello, 1984.

449.   García, Oscar. *Controles utilizados en la distribución y recepción del material censal y en el flujo de los cuestionarios hacia el sistema de procesamiento de datos: Venezuela.* Caracas: Oficina Central de Estadística e Informática, 1986.
        Description of the different stages in the flow of census materials in the 1981 census: production, packing, shipping, distribution, revision, archiving, processing. The last stage is discussed in particular detail.

450.   Heinen, Heinz Dieter. "El censo indígena entre los warao: operación de campo, evaluación y resultados preliminares." In: Haydee Seijas, ed. *Aportes a la investigación censal de la población indígena de Venezuela.* In press.
        Methodology and evaluation of the 1982 Indian census as carried out for one particular tribe, with preliminary results.

451.   Osorio Alvarez, Emilio A. *Geografía de la población de Venezuela.* Caracas: Editorial Ariel-Seix Barral Venezolana, 1985.
        Contains a section describing the official censuses 1873-1936.

452.   Páez Celis, Julio. "Consideraciones acerca de la calidad de los datos demográficos de Venezuela." In: Gabriel Bidegain Greising, ed. *Estado actual de los estudios de la población en Venezuela.* Caracas: Instituto Latinoamericano de Investigaciones Sociales, and Universidad Católica Andrés Bello, 1987.
        Contains evaluations of all the national population censuses of Venezuela since 1873.

453.   Seijas, Haydee. "El censo indígena de Venezuela de 1982: metodología, operación y resultados globales." Paper presented at the XXXIII annual convention of the Asociación Venezolana para el Avance de la Ciencia. Caracas, October 1983.

454.   _____; Suels, M. E.; Lizarralde, R.; et al. "Datos censales preliminares de la población indígena de las comunidades y colectividades de la cuenca del Orinoco y zonas adyacentes." Paper presented at the XXXIV annual convention of the Asociación Venezolana para el Avance de la Ciencia. Cumaná, November 1984.

455.   Venezuela. Dirección General de Estadística y Censos Nacionales. *Segundo censo experimental de población y vivienda, ciudad de Valera.* Caracas, 1980.
        Census documentation includes questionnaire and several manuals, in five separate documents.

456. Venezuela. Oficina Central de Estadística e Informática. *XI censo general de población y vivienda, 20 de octubre de 1981. Censos 1950-1981. Población total por entidades federales, distritos y municipios, sexo y grupos de edad.* Caracas, 1983.

Second part consists of sample census for 1981 national census. Methodology and basic concepts are briefly discussed.

457. _____. *XI censo general de población y vivienda, 20 de octubre de 1981. Total regional.* Caracas, 1985.

A detailed introduction has chapters on the census history of Venezuela; the structure and organization of the 1981 census; basis concepts and definitions; a list of professional classifications used; analysis of the results. Limited information on methodology.

458. _____. *Programa censal 1980.* Caracas, 1983. (Mimeo.)

A seven-volume collection of manuals to be used in the 1981 census.

459. Venezuela. Oficina Central de Estadística e Informática. Censo Indígena. *XI censo general de población y vivienda. Censo indígena.* Caracas, 1982-1985.

Census of indigenous population. Documentation (manuals, list of Indian communities, etc.) includes description of operational details such as training of personnel, sample questionnaires, concepts and definitions, evaluation of data, analysis of results.

460. Villalon, M. E. "La población y las comunidades E'ñapa según el censo indígena de 1982: resumen e interpretación etnográfica de algunos datos censales." In: Haydee Seijas, ed. *Aportes a la investigación censal de la población indígena de Venezuela.* In press.

Author Index

Author Index

Altmann, Ana Maria Goldani, 211
Alvarado Franquiz, Juan, 426
Alvarez, Leonel, 259
Arana Sialer, Andrés, 366
Arboleda Camargo, Henrique, 304
Arca Parró, Alberto, 369, 370, 371, 372, 373, 374
Archer, Alford, 10
Ardissone, Romualdo, 71
Argentina
    Comisión Directiva del Censo, 64
    Comisión Nacional del Censo, 69
    Consejo Federal de Inversiones. Biblioteca, 87
    Dirección General del Servicio Estadístico Nacional, 75, 76, 86
    Government, 48
    Instituto Nacional de Estadística y Censos, 49, 50, 104, 105, 112, 115
Arias, Alfonso R., 235
Arretx, Carmen, 51
Arrias, A., 440
Asociación Colombiana para el Estudio de la Población, 305
Associação Brasileira de Estudos Populacionais, 223, 224, 225
Averanga Mollinedo, Asthenio, 142

Balhana, Altiva Pilatti, 212
Banguero Lozano, Harold, 319
Barros, Ernani T. de, 213
Batschelet, Clarence E., 10
Bayona Nuñez, Alberto, 306
Bercovich, Alicia M., 226
Bermeo C., Jack, 332
Bernacchi, Margarita, 116
Besio Moreno, Nicolás, 72, 77
Bidegain Greising, Gabriel, 448
Boggio, Juan M., 427
Boleda, Mario, 117
Bolivia
    Dirección General de Estadística, 136
    Dirección General de Estadística y Censos, 139, 141
    Dirección Nacional de Estadística, 134
    Instituto Nacional de Estadística, 143, 144, 145, 146, 147, 148, 150, 151, 152, 153, 154
    Oficina Nacional de Inmigración, Estadística y Propaganda Geográfica, 135
Borges, T. P. Accioly, 207
Braga, André Duarte, 161

Brazil
    Directoria Geral de Estatística, 159, 160
    Fundação Instituto Brasileiro de Geografia e Estatística, 34, 208, 214, 215,
        216, 217, 227, 228, 229, 230
    Instituto Brasileiro de Geografia e Estatística, 162, 163, 164, 165, 166, 167,
        168, 184, 185, 186, 187, 188, 189, 190, 191, 192, 193, 194, 195, 196, 197,
        198, 199, 200, 201, 202
    Ministério do Trabalho, Indústria e Comércio, 169
Buenos Aires (City), Argentina, 62, 65, 70, 73
Buenos Aires (Province), Argentina, 63

Camacho Villarroel, Miriam, 158
Camisa, Zulma C., 88
Canadian International Development Agency, 50
Canton, Dario, 106
Carruyo, D., 440
Cataldi, Alberto, 89
Cavallini, Carlos, 155
Celedón, Juan Vicente, 270
Centro de Estudios de Población y Desarrollo, Peru, 389
Centro Latinoamericano de Demografía, 11, 12, 18, 19, 30, 50, 154, 411
Cerisola, M. J. Elsa, 90
Chackiel, Juan, 51
Charry Lara, Alberto, 293
Chen, Chi-Yi, 441
Chile
    Dirección de Estadística y Censos, 260, 261, 262, 263
    Dirección General de Estadística, 244, 246, 247, 248
    Dirección Nacional de Estadística, 249, 250, 251, 255
    Instituto Nacional de Estadísticas, 271, 272, 276, 277
    Junta Gubernativa, 256
    Oficina Central de Estadística, 239, 240, 241, 242
    Servicio Nacional de Estadística y Censos, 257
Cirigliano, Antonio, 91
Colombia
    Departamento Administrativo Nacional de Estadística, 294, 295, 301, 307,
        308, 309, 310, 311, 312, 313, 314, 323, 324, 325, 326
    Dirección General de Estadística, 283, 284
    Dirección Nacional de Estadística, 287, 288, 296
    Ministerio de Gobierno, 282
Cordi de Cuevas, Angela, 318
Cortés, Rosalia, 118
Corvalán, Graziella, 357
Costa, Luiz N. da, 231
Costa, Tereza Cristina N. Aráujo, 218
Crocco Ferrari, Juan, 252
Cruchaga, Miguel, 245
Cruz-Coke, R., 264
Cuadra, Guillermo de la, 253

Dagnino Pastore, Lorenzo, 79
Dehollain, Alejandro, 92, 259
Dieulefait, Carlos E., 74
Domschke, Eliane, 52
Duenas Cabrera, Julio, 396

Echeverri Perrico, Rafael, 328
Ecuador
    Dirección General de Estadística, 330
    Dirección General de Estadística y Censos, 335
    Instituto Nacional de Estadística y Censos, 342, 343, 346, 347
    Junta Nacional de Planificación y Coordinación. División de Estadística y Censos, 336
    Núcleo de Estadísticos del Ecuador. Comisión de Censos, 333
    Oficina de los Censos Nacionales, 344
Elizalde, María Laura, 119

Fajardo Montaña, Dario, 315
Felippe, José Carneiro, 170
Fernández, Alfredo, 404
Fernández Baca de Valdez, Graciela, 397
Fernández Medrano, Julio, 158
Fernández Pernas, José, 120
Ferreira, Carlos Eugenio de C., 211
Ferro Calvo, Mauricio, 327
Figueiredo, Jaime de, 203
Florez Nieto, Carmen Elisa, 318, 328
Fogel, Ramón, 357
Fuentes, Manuel A., 362

Galeano, Luis A., 355
García, María Nieves, 121
García, Oscar, 449
García Castro, Arturo G., 329
García Frias, R., 375
García Rosquellas, R., 137
Gauld, Charles A., 171
Gómez, Fernando, 302, 316
González R., L. E., 317
González Villalobos, Alvaro, 116, 122
Goyer, Doreen S., 52
Griva, Edelmi E., 107
Gutiérrez Roldán, Héctor, 265, 273

Hamerley, Michael T., 345
Hasselmann, Sergio, 209
Heinen, Heinz Dieter, 450
Hernández García, Alberto, 318
Herrera, Gonzalo, 367
Herrera Malpica, Nestor, 31

Higuita, Juan de Dios, 289
Hugon, Paul, 219

Instituto Alejandro E. Bunge de Investigaciones Económicas y Sociales, Argentina, 80
Instituto de Pesquizas Econômicas, Brazil, 232
Inter-American Statistical Institute, Washington, D.C., 2, 3, 13, 14, 15, 16, 20, 21, 22, 32, 33, 34, 81, 140, 274, 297, 337, 434
Irwin, Richard, 220
Isea Leonardi, Pedro, 31, 40

Jamaica. University of the West Indies. Census Research Programme, 349
James, Preston E., 1
Jiménez Castro, Wilburg, 405

Kappes Barrientos, Héctor, 266
Kegler de Galeano, Anneliese, 354
Keyfitz, Nathan, 93
Klaczko, Jaime, 416
Kritz, Ernesto H., 123

Lassus Arevalo, Carlos E., 376, 377
Lattes, Alfredo E., 94, 95, 101
Lehwing, Mariene Bougeard, 233
Library of Congress Census Library Project, 4
Lindenboim, Javier, 124
Lizarralde, R., 454
Lleras Restrepo, Carlos, 285
Llorens, Emilio, 82
Lopes, Valdecir Freire, 23, 35, 36, 53
López Toro, Alvaro, 303
Loyo González, Gilberto, 5
Luna Vegas, Ricardo, 6, 7, 378, 379

Maeder, Ernesto J. A., 96, 97, 98, 99
Magallanes Territory, Argentina, 243
Mamalakis, Markos, 278
Marcilio, Maria-Luiza, 210
Marks, Eli S., 266
Martine, George, 234, 235
Masferrer, Elio, 37
Mattelart, Armand, 267
Mayer, Enrique, 37
McCaa, Robert, 275
Medica, Vilma, 156
Medici, André C., 236
Melgarejo Rey, Jesús M., 298
Mellon, Roger, 352
Mendez Heilman, Regina, 319
Mendive, Pedro, 8

Mendoza (Province), Argentina
    Ministerio de Economía, Obras Públicas y Riego, 83
Merlo Jaramillo, Pedro, 338
Merrick, Thomas William, 237
Mexico, Government, 48
Meyer, Morton A., 405
Mezza Rosso, Victor, 157
Miller, Juan E., 406
Minujin, Alberto, 125
Miró, Carmen, 24, 25
Misiones (Province), Argentina
    Dirección General de Estadística, 100
    Dirección General de Estadística y Censos, 108, 109
Monteagudo, Emilio, 84
Montenegro, Tulio Hostilio, 26
Montoya, Hernán, 290
Morales Vergara, Julio, 258, 268
Moreira, Maxwell Ribeiro, 54
Moreno, José Luís, 106
Moreno, Martín, 31, 132, 133
Mortara, Giorgio, 27, 172, 173, 174, 175, 176, 177, 178, 179, 180, 204, 205, 206

Nieto T., Bolívar, 339
Novaro de Cosarinsky, Sara, 116

O'Brien, Donald J., 8
Ochoa, Elena de, 435
Olivares, Juan, 320
Ordoñez, Myriam, 321
Orsatti, Alvaro, 126
Ortiz, José C., 353
Ortiz C., Luis B., 299
Ortiz Mejía, Corina del Pilar, 348
Osorio Alvarez, Emilio A., 451

Packer, Abel, 55
Páez Celis, Julio, 436, 437, 452
Palau Viladesau, Tomás, 355
Pantelides, Edith A., 39, 127
Paraguay
    Dirección General de Estadística y Censos, 356, 359, 360
    Dirección Nacional de Estadística, 350
    Instituto Paraguayo del Indígena, 361
Paz Soldán, Mariano Felipe, 363
Paz y Miño, Luis T., 331
Pereira Salas, Eugenio, 269
Peru
    Consejo Nacional de Población, 398
    Dirección General de Censos, Encuestas y Demografía, 390
    Dirección Nacional de Estadística, 380, 381, 382

Dirección Nacional de Estadística y Censos, 388
Instituto Nacional de Estadística, 391, 399, 400, 401
Ministerio de Fomento, 364, 365
Oficina Nacional de Estadística, 392, 393
Oficina Nacional de Estadística y Censos, 394, 395
Pessoa, H. E. Alvim, 181
Petrucelli, José L., 412
Picouet, Michel, 441
Pizzi, Mario, 435
Poczter, R., 95
Potter, Joseph, 321

Quick, Sylvia, 322

Reátegui, H. Ladislao, 368
Rey Riveros, Edmundo, 387
Rial Roade, Juan, 417, 418
Rio Grande do Sul (State), Brazil
        Fundação de Economia e Estatística, 238
Rivarola, Domingo M., 357
Rivas González, Ernesto, 40
Rodríguez, Manuel Alfredo, 442
Rojas Molina, Omar, 407
Rosario (City), Argentina, 67, 68
Ruiz Guzmán, Sonia, 443

Salvia, F., 92
Sánchez-Albornoz, Nicolás, 41
Santiana, Antonio, 334
Saunders, J. V. D., 340
Seijas, Haydee, 453, 454
Silva, Ari N., 56, 57
Silvero, Arnaldo, 352
Soares, José C. de Macedo, 182, 183
Somoza, Jorge L., 42, 92, 101, 128, 129
Soroco, Carlos, 138
Spielman, Evelyn, 220
Stessin, Laurence, 383
Stockwell, Edward G., 43
Stycos, J. Mayone, 28
Suárez, María Matilde, 448
Suárez Rivadeneira, Antonio, 286, 291
Suels, M. E., 454

Tacia Chamy, Odette, 279, 280
Torrado, Susana, 44, 58, 59, 60
Torrez Pinto, Hugo, 149
Travis, Carole, 281

United Nations
    Economic Commission for Latin America, 45, 46, 47, 61, 154, 341
    Statistical Office, 17
    Technical Assistance Administration, 29
United States
    Office of Inter-American Affairs, 9
Universidad de Buenos Aires
    Instituto de Sociología, 78
Universidad de la República de Uruguay
    Instituto de Estadística, 413
Uriarte, Carlos A., 384, 385
Uruguay
    Dirección General de Estadística y Censos, 419, 420, 421, 422,423
    Dirección Nacional de Estadística y Censos, 408, 409, 414, 415
    Junta Asesora de Estadística y Censos, 410

Vaccaro, Juan M., 85
Vapñarsky, César A., 102, 103, 110, 130
Vasconcellos, Mauricio Teixeira Leite de, 233
Veloso, Heitor C., 221
Venegas Borges, Pedro Luis, 444
Venezuela
    Dirección General de Estadística, 425, 428, 429, 430, 431
    Dirección General de Estadística y Censos Nacionales, 432, 433, 438, 439,
        445, 455
    Oficina Central de Estadística e Informática, 446, 447, 456, 457, 458
    Oficina Central de Estadística e Informática. Censo Indígena, 459
Vergara, Roberto, 254
Vidal Z., David E., 158
Viglione de Arrastia, Hebe, 111
Vildosolo, Reyes, 435
Villalon, M. E., 460

Wainerman, Catalina H., 131, 132, 133
Westphalen, Cecília Maria, 212
Wicks, Jerry W., 43
Williams, John H., 358

Young, Drew M., 222

Zalamea, Jorge, 292
Zavala, Graciela, 386
Zubieta, Hernando, 300
Zúñiga, Luís, 60